I0410424

THE U.S. RESPONSE TO NORTH KOREA'S NUCLEAR PROVOCATIONS

HEARING

BEFORE THE

SUBCOMMITTEE ON ASIA AND THE PACIFIC

OF THE

COMMITTEE ON FOREIGN AFFAIRS
HOUSE OF REPRESENTATIVES

ONE HUNDRED FOURTEENTH CONGRESS

SECOND SESSION

JANUARY 13, 2016

Serial No. 114–148

Printed for the use of the Committee on Foreign Affairs

Available via the World Wide Web: http://www.foreignaffairs.house.gov/ or
http://www.gpo.gov/fdsys/

U.S. GOVERNMENT PUBLISHING OFFICE

98–313PDF   WASHINGTON : 2016

For sale by the Superintendent of Documents, U.S. Government Publishing Office
Internet: bookstore.gpo.gov   Phone: toll free (866) 512–1800; DC area (202) 512–1800
Fax: (202) 512–2104   Mail: Stop IDCC, Washington, DC 20402–0001

CONTENTS

THE U.S. RESPONSE TO NORTH KOREA'S NUCLEAR PROVOCATIONS

WEDNESDAY, JANUARY 13, 2016

House of Representatives,
Subcommittee on Asia and the Pacific,
Committee on Foreign Affairs,
Washington, DC.

The subcommittee met, pursuant to notice, at 9 o'clock a.m., in room 2172 Rayburn House Office Building, Hon. Matt Salmon (chairman of the subcommittee) presiding.

Mr. SALMON. On the evening of January 6, North Korea likely conducted its fourth nuclear weapons test. North Korean leader Kim Jong Un claimed that the test was a fusion reactive hydrogen bomb. Most experts are skeptical, given seismic evidence and North Korea's penchant for overstatement. But it is, nonetheless, incredibly concerning.

We convene this hearing today not only to join the international community in condemning the test, but to work to find a feasible lasting solution to address the North Korean nuclear threat.

For many in the United States, if we think of North Korea it is usually the butt of a joke, reference to either The Interview or Team America movies. Despite repeated calls from both respectable civilian thinkers and top military leadership citing North Korea as a top threat in the Pacific theater, North Korea seems to have been off the Obama administration's radar.

Instead, they have dismissed the imminent threat by employing its so-called "strategy of patience"—or, excuse me, "strategic patience." For our allies in the region, North Korean provocations mean so much more, and it should for the United States as well.

History has proven that North Korea has every intention to continue advancing its nuclear program. In an effort to strengthen both domestic and international positions, the United States has shown a willingness to negotiate with North Korea if it is simply willing to first take steps toward denuclearization. North Korea has shown no interest in doing so, but it has successfully extracted food assistance and other foreign assistance from us by threatening nuclear activity. This is an unacceptable cycle that cannot continue.

Due to North Korea's nuclear threat and proximity to our allies, South Korea, and Japan, our response options are limited, but they largely fall into two categories—sanctions and information flow. Some argue for United Nations sanctions, but others say that would exert little pressure on North Korea, largely due to China's lack of enforcement. Some speak of North Korea as the most heavily sanctioned state in the world, but that is simply not the case.

For example, Iran is subject to sanctions under 18 U.S. executive orders, and North Korea is subject to six. I applaud Chairman Royce for his work on the North Korea sanctions legislation which passed the House yesterday. I am proud to vote for that, and I think it is a good start. But I think much more to be done, and that is why we are here today.

China's relationships with North Korea continues to be a problem. China favors North Korea's status quo over the demise of the Kim regime, which it fears could mean a unified United States allied Korea as a neighbor and a sizeable flood of refugees crossing their border.

These vested interests are why China continues to prop up this pariah state with food, oil, and assistance. I am deeply disappointed that China continues to allow North Korea to destabilize the region in this manner. China must tighten sanctions and really enforce the sanctions that are in place and apply the unique pressure that only it—North Korea's patron—can provide.

While a nuclear test quickly draws the world's attention toward North Korean leadership, we must remember that there are 24 million people living in this closed-off state, starved of basic necessities. Furthermore, citizens are brainwashed into believing that their leadership is actually helping them.

The North Korean Human Rights Act of 2004 initiated radio broadcasting to provide basic knowledge of the outside world to the people of North Korea. Twelve years have since passed and technological advances have been made, and our policies should reflect that reality. I intend to introduce legislation that would update this program this provide greater, more useful information to inform and empower their citizens.

In 2006, North Korea was removed from the State Sponsor of Terrorism List in an attempt to bring it to the negotiation table and ultimately halt its nuclear program. Congress has debated this issue, and many members believe it should be put back on the list. Count me in that category.

Given the Sony cyberattacks, the shelling of South Korean ships, North Korea's alleged ties to Hamas, Hezbollah, and Iran, and now this fourth nuclear test, perhaps—maybe perhaps nuclear should be placed back on the list.

The leaders of North Korea, as well as China, should understand that every Pyongyang provocation will induce a congressional response in an attempt to alter North Korea's ways. There is calamity across the globe blurring our focus, but the Obama administration's employment of ''strategic patience'' comes, I believe, at our peril. Let's be done with ''strategic patience.'' It is time for strategic clarity. We must be proactive in our efforts, and I look forward to this important discussion of any recommendations this distinguished panel can offer.

Members present will be permitted to submit written statements to be included in the official hearing record. And without objection, the hearing record will remain open for 5 calendar days to allow statements, questions, and extraneous materials for the record, subject to the length limitation in the rules.

And I would like to turn the time over to the ranking member for any comments that he might make.

Mr. SHERMAN. Thank you. North Korea probably tested a hydrogen-boosted device, one that made use of hydrogen isotopes but did not get its power from the fusion of hydrogen atoms. That being said, it is perhaps half a decade or a decade before North Korea tests a genuine thermonuclear weapon. I am sure our witnesses will be able to clarify and give us a more precise estimate.

We have throughout this century, which is now in its 16th year, had a policy which has completely failed us as foreign policy, but has achieved what some would argue is the guiding force behind foreign policy, which is meeting domestic political concerns. We have not—neither the last administration nor this administration— slowed down North Korea's nuclear program for any significant time, and continuing this policy, or repeating what we have done but only in a louder voice, is not going to yield a different result.

But our policy has allowed us at times—for various times—to seem tough, and we have avoided offending Wall Street. These are important domestic political objectives which have been fully achieved. So if viewed from the standpoint of being popular domestically, our policy is a success. If we want to protect the world from North Korean nuclear weapons, it has been a complete failure.

In terms of what we could do if sounding tough wasn't important, we could make it clear to China that, if there was a unified Korea, American forces would not be north of the 38th parallel and might even be further south. There would be less reason for them to be there.

We do not have any military forces defending any other China neighbor from China. Our troops in South Korea are there to defend South Korea from North Korea. We could offer North Korea a package of aid—that has been done before—but a non-aggression pact that they asked for and we refused to provide, because Dick Cheney imagined invasion, or at least didn't want to give up that opportunity sometime in the future.

But the most important thing we need to do, and the thing we are least likely to do, is to make it clear to China that their access to U.S. markets depends upon them getting tough with North Korea. Wall Street would be aghast if we actually did it, so we won't. So we are likely to continue the current circumstance. China is indeed miffed by what North Korea has done, but is unwilling to change its policy, and, of course, China has been miffed by North Korea many times in the past.

China will not change its policy unless the reality changes, and the current reality is they have free access to U.S. markets and that won't be changed if they choose to continue the policy that they have continued throughout this century, which is to subsidize North Korea.

So if we want a policy that doesn't meet domestic political objectives, but simply maximizes the carrots and sticks on North Korea, it would be a matter of a non-aggression pact on the 38th parallel, and the threat of tariffs on Chinese goods if China continues— while always questioning—it but continues a policy of subsidizing North Korea.

So my guess is that we will simply continue to pull our hair out—obviously, I have done more of that than most of the witnesses—in worry about North Korea, and talk tough, and do nothing that offends Wall Street. And if you keep doing the same thing for now a 16-year-old century, and expect a different result, that is the definition of insanity.

And a final thing I will ask our witnesses to comment on is whether we would actually get somewhere if we consent—if we agreed that North Korea could have a very limited number of atomic but not thermonuclear weapons, or is there a real prospect of getting them to be a nuclear-free state.

I yield back.

Mr. SALMON. I just wanted to comment for the ranking member, I think that many of the issues that you raised are thought-provoking and reasonable, and I would like to extend a hand across the partisan divide to work with you in any way, shape, or form to not just pull our hair out but actually get some results.

And if that offends some folks, some special interests, then so be it. I think the more important goal is to have success. I think all of the world expects success. And so I just want to say that I think you have raised some legitimate issues that need to be explored, and I intend to work with you to do that. Look forward to it.

Mr. Rohrabacher.

Mr. ROHRABACHER. Thank you very much, Mr. Chairman, and thank you for holding this hearing at a very significant moment.

Our relations with both Koreas go back a long way, and I have a long memory. I still remember sitting right here in this room when the Clinton administration was proposing to us that we have—that we cut a deal, basically, with North Korea, that we would be providing them food and fuel for an agreement not to do what they apparently have been doing, which is—I don't care if you want to call it a hydrogen booster device or a hydrogen nuclear weapon; the fact is they obviously have been spending their money on developing ways of mass murdering other people while we have been providing them the money for their food and fuel.

To say that that is absolutely unacceptable is to put it mildly. And, at that time, I indicated, and several other Republicans, I might add, and a couple of other Democrats as well, I might add, pointed out that that is what would happen, and here it has. Surprise, surprise. They have used their resources to develop weapons of mass destruction. We have subsidized them in using our money to provide them food and fuel, which should be coming out of their, how do you say, hydrogen boosting device development budget.

Let me suggest that this nuclear explosion, and the continued—the obvious continued work that North Korea is doing on nuclear military devices, that should at least put us into a mindset that we have to do something different than what we have been doing.

And let me note that President Abe of Japan has made it very, very clear that there are threats to the Pacific, and I would applaud President Abe for reaching out to South Korea at this moment. President Abe of Japan has gone the extra mile to address sensitivities in South Korea that are left over way from World War II.

And he needs to be applauded for that, and he needs to also be encouraged to rebuild Japan's military strength, so that he can work with the United States of America in preserving the peace in that part of the world, instead of having the United States having to carry the entire load on our own.

So with that said, I would finish by saying the other factor is, which the chairman mentioned, China. Just as it was obvious that the North Korea regime, as corrupt and belligerent and as repressive as it is, would be using their money to develop weapons while we provided them food and fuel, it is just as evident that they have a relationship with Beijing that puts Beijing into a position of influence in North Korea, if not dominance of North Korea.

So let us, again, to the point that we applaud President Abe for reaching out and policies that are going to ultimately bring more stability to that part of the world, let us condemn Beijing for not using its influence in a way that would bring more stability and peace to that region.

So we need to work together on this, and, Mr. Chairman, thank you for calling this hearing. Looking forward to hearing for specifics and information from the witnesses that will help us develop our policy now as we start into this new era.

Thank you.

Mr. SALMON. I thank the gentleman from California.

Mr. Bera.

Mr. BERA. Thank you, Mr. Chairman, and thank you for the timeliness of this hearing. A few weeks ago I had a chance to visit the Republic of Korea, visit with our troops, and spend a few days around Christmas with our troops, also visiting with the Korean foreign secretaries, national security folks, et cetera.

I also had a chance to go up to the demilitarized zone and, you know, chat with our troops, see the Republic of Korea troops. The demilitarized zone is an oxymoron. This is one of the most heavily militarized zones in the world, and it is a constant reminder that we are in a cease fire. we are not in a state of peace.

You know, listening to the remarks of my colleagues, I think it is important for us to learn from what we have tried in the past, and so forth. But the conundrum is North Korea is not easy, and it will require a partnership with the countries in that region.

And, in many cases, we all land at the same place, that China really does have to take a leadership role here. China is the one country that does have some leverage with North Korea, but it will take a partnership between, you know, the Chinese Government, the Russians, Japan, our Korean allies, along with U.S. leadership, in order to address this.

It is in all of our interest to deescalate tensions, to try to bring North Korea into the 21st century. And the other goal that I think many Koreans have of seeing reunification, you know, it is not going to be easy. It will take world leadership. It will take the nations, along with the United States, in that region working together, but it can be done if we put our minds to it. And we have to; there is an urgency now, as indicated by the recent North Korean nuclear tests.

It is complicated, and, you know, the President talked about the threats that, you know, we face in the Middle East. But those are not threats to our very existence as a nation, and North Korea, with the hydrogen bomb, with ballistic missile and ICBM capabilities, are a threat to world stability, and we have got to direct this. There is the urgency of now.

And, Mr. Chairman, I look forward to working with you to kind of navigate this path forward, and it is incredibly important.

Mr. SALMON. Thank you.

Mr. Chabot.

Mr. CHABOT. Thank you very much, and thank you, Mr. Chairman, for holding this important hearing. I mean, there is no question that the world has had a problem for a long time with respect to North Korea, particularly their leadership. Whether the grandfather or the father or the son now, they are all equally as crazy, I am afraid, particularly the newest one.

But their own people continue to suffer and to starve. They are the most politically isolated country on the globe. Despite that, they continue—they have absolute contempt for most of the rest of the world, including their neighbors. And with this fourth now in the last number of years nuclear tests, and we have reason to believe it is hydrogen, although that hasn't been confirmed necessarily yet, but, nonetheless, it is terribly disturbing.

I think every administration, from the Clinton administration to the Bush administration to the Obama administration has failed with respect to North Korea, and that is most unfortunate. And now with the increasing sophistication of their missile systems, the United States is at risk as well. But two countries that are even more at risk at, obviously, South Korea and Japan.

And as my colleague, Mr. Rohrabacher from California indicated, China is the key here. China is the only country that has any real influence over North Korea. And the only thing that is going to get China's attention is if those two countries, Japan and South Korea, seriously consider nuclear programs of their own. That is the only thing that is going to get China's attention. It is the last thing China wants.

And so I would urge those two countries to think seriously about this. I am not encouraging them to do it, but even thinking about it and discussing it I think will get China's attention. And maybe China will finally act to put the pressure on North Korea necessary to get them to back off this insanity of one of the poorest countries in the world spending all their money on nuclear weaponry to threaten the rest of the world.

I yield back, Mr. Chairman.

Mr. SALMON. I thank the gentleman. Is there anybody else that seeks recognition on the panel before—yes, Mr. Lowenthal.

Mr. LOWENTHAL. Thank you, Mr. Chair, for holding this hearing. I find this very interesting. I think the focus of what you have heard a lot is China, what are we going to do to deal with China in terms of the pressure that China has. To me, there are a couple of questions I would like to understand before we get into what we have to do to press China, or to do anything else; that is, what does China want? Where is China at this—not because of our pressure.

Two, I have seen over the past year or so some articles, especially in the New York Times, about Chinese officials, former military officials, retired, talking about the unsustainability of the Kim regime, and that there is a real concern in China about instability in North Korea. I would like to hear that discussion, that there is going to be pressure from the bottom up. People cannot live under those conditions, and the Chinese know this. The Chinese know, and there are real worries about the Chinese, about what that instability is going to lead to in terms of them.

So that leads us to the third point; that is, when we talk about China, knowing that China—it is not getting China involved. China is very involved with what are the consequences. It may have its own agenda about what it wants to do with this. The question is, besides pressure on China—and we have heard a lot, and I am not saying that that is not a potential—what are the ways of partnership with China? What do you see as the opportunities at this moment to be dealing with?

Thank you very much, and I yield back.

Mr. SALMON. I thank Mr. Lowenthal. Very insightful thoughts and questions.

If there are no other opening statements, then I am going to move to the panel, first of all introducing three great experts on this dicey issue. First is Dr. Victor Cha, senior adviser and Korea chair at the Center for Strategic and International Studies. It is good to see you again, Dr. Cha. Mr. Bruce Klingner, senior research fellow for Northeast Asia at The Heritage Foundation. And Ms. Bonnie Glaser, who is the senior adviser for Asia and director of the China Power Project at the Center for Strategic and International Studies.

We are thrilled to have all of you here today, and thank you for making the time available. First, I will introduce Dr. Cha.

STATEMENT OF VICTOR CHA, PH.D., SENIOR ADVISER AND KOREA CHAIR, CENTER FOR STRATEGIC AND INTERNATIONAL STUDIES

Mr. CHA. Thank you, Mr. Chairman, Representative Sherman, and members of the committee. It really is an honor to speak to you today about a very difficult topic, and that is North Korea.

You mentioned—both the chairman and Congressman Bera mentioned urgency, and I think there is a great deal of urgency. There are elements of deterrence and crisis instability that derive from North Korea's nuclear weapons status that I don't think the North Koreans fully comprehend. And it can also be the case that the North Korean leader, this young North Korean leader, views nuclear weapons as usable weapons rather than as strategic elements of deterrence, valuable only in their non-use.

So the urgency is that the result could be a disaster at the cost of tens of thousands of lives, at which point the world is going to wonder why the United States did nothing to stop this before it was too late.

So what have we done? In the administration's own words, strategic patience, the policy of strategic patience, had two objectives. The first was to break the cycle of provocations for negotiations that was the flaw of past administration's policies.

Second, the concept was that this idea of pressure and non-dialogue would eventually cause the North Koreans to feel compelled to come back to negotiations genuinely willing to cut a deal. When this did not work, the administration did try to reach out and engage, but all of these offers had been spurned by the regime.

So we are in the worst of all worlds right now. There is no diplomacy. There are more tests, a growing program, a new cycle of provocations. We have had four nuclear tests, three of them during the Obama administration, two of them before the President's State of the Union speech. And at the rate we are going, this issue is just going to get punted to the next administration, and it is going to be an exponentially worse problem.

So a new approach to North Korea has to focus on what Bob Gallucci and I described in the New York Times last week as asymmetric pressure points. In my experience, being involved in the negotiations in the previous administration, there were only two times where I felt like the North Koreans were truly caught off guard, uncertain of how to respond.

The first of these was in September 2005 when the Treasury Department took actions that led to the freezing of North Korean assets at a bank in China. And the second was in February 2014 in the aftermath of the United Nations Commission of Inquiry report of which the major recommendation was referral of the North Korean leadership to the ICC for crimes against humanity.

These were the only two times that I really felt the North Koreans were frazzled, and I think a new strategy has to build on these pressure points. Let me just highlight a couple of these.

First is sanctions, and I know Bruce will talk about this as well. As the chairman said, it is a policy myth that North Korea is the most sanctioned country in the world, and the chairman cited some of the statistics for how the sanctioning against Iran is much higher than that against North Korea. So there is plenty more space to operate there.

Secondary sanctioning should also be given positive consideration. I know that this has been talked about within policy circles as a significant escalation, and this will certainly complicate our relationships with China, the European Union, Southeast Asia, South America, and Africa. But it is also certain that many of these entities will comply when given the choice of dealing with North Korea or losing access to the U.S. financial system.

We should also give serious consideration, as the chairman said, to putting North Korea back on the State Sponsor of Terrorism List. I know that there will be lawyers who will dispute the legal criteria for putting North Korea back on the list, and here I would only urge that particular attention be given to North Korea's cyber capabilities. We did research at CSIS that shows that the activities, these cyber activities, are instigated by the same agencies, entities within the North Korean Government that have been responsible in the past for terrorist acts.

Human rights has to complement sanctions as part of an asymmetric strategy. One of the potential targets would be North Korean slave labor. There are over 50,000 workers in Africa, the Middle East, Europe, Russia, and China, that are operating in subhuman conditions that are being paid nothing. Their revenues all are going back to the North Korean Government. There are different estimates, between $250 million to over $2 billion of hard currency. So this is certainly something that should be targeted.

Another useful asymmetric pressure point is the Kaesong Industrial Complex. This project now provides $90 million in hard currency to North Korean authorities, with little wages actually going back to the factory workers. The South Korean Government will probably be opposed to something like this, because even conservative governments have grown attached to the Kaesong industrial complex, but difficult times call for difficult measures.

Lastly, on information, North Korea under Kim has proven to be hypersensitive to external criticism with renewal of the North Korean Human Rights Act, and I entirely agree with the chairman on the idea of trying to increase funding and basically think about new ways of bringing information into the country.

As some of the work that we have done with the Bush Institute has shown, the United States and South Korea can come up with a comprehensive strategy for breaking down North Korean information barriers, because in the end we need to improve the human condition of the people in North Korea.

Thank you very much.

[The prepared statement of Mr. Cha follows:]

CSIS | CENTER FOR STRATEGIC & INTERNATIONAL STUDIES

Statement before the

House Committee on Foreign Affairs

Subcommittee on Asia and the Pacific

"The U.S. Response to North Korea's Nuclear Provocations"

A Testimony by:

Dr. Victor D. Cha

Professor of Government, Georgetown University

Senior Adviser and Korea Chair, Center for Strategic and International Studies

and Fellow in Human Freedom, George W. Bush Institute

January 13, 2016

2172 Rayburn House Office Building

WWW.CSIS.ORG   1616 RHODE ISLAND AVENUE NW   TEL. (202) 887.0200
WASHINGTON, DC 20036   FAX (202) 775.3199

Chairman Salmon, Representative Sherman (ranking Democrat) and distinguished members of the committee, it is a distinct honor to appear before this committee to discuss the challenges posed by North Korea and the U.S. response to this threat.

As Bob Gallucci and I argued in the *New York Times* last Friday, there is a path forward for the U.S. after the fourth nuclear test. I would like to start off with the same quote that we used in that op-ed, where a North Korean diplomat unintentionally offered us a valuable insight into his country's nuclear policy. That diplomat, in 2005, said: "The reason you attacked Afghanistan is because they don't have nukes. And look at what happened to Libya. That is why we will never give up ours."

Now flash forward to 2016. The North Koreans can point to Libya again in 2011, and to Syria in the past year to defend the necessity of their nuclear program. Kim Jong-un himself is probably feeling pretty comfortable and secure believing that he has the ultimate insurance policy, a nuclear weapons program his father started, and one that he has spent considerable resources to develop since taking over four years ago.

But therein lies the problem. Kim Jong-un believes that a bigger and more modern nuclear arsenal purchases him more security by deterring others from attacking him despite anything he might do. That belief is deadly wrong, dangerous, and could cost many lives. Successes and improvements in the nuclear and the missile program in the past few years, moreover, may have inflated that self-belief, to a point where a miscalculation, potentially in the form of "grey zone" coercive military action at lower levels of escalation like the sinking of a ROK or U.S. ship to extort food or benefits, can lead to retaliation. The most worrying thing about North Korea today is not that it did a fourth nuclear test last week, but that it does not recognize the limitations and risks the nuclear program poses. His false confidence could well start a war with an angry Seoul that will respond kinetically to future acts of violence.

How do we convince a rogue regime, run by a young, insecure and inexperienced leader with a penchant for big nukes and expensive weapons systems that he cannot develop both nuclear weapons and the economy at the same time? And how do we convince him that he must give up his weapons in order to bring genuine economic reforms and changes to a long suffering country?

Distinguished members of the committee, I bring before you today three sets of comments that hopefully will offer a window for the U.S. to help solve that problem. The first is to recognize the threat posed by North Korea; the second is to sketch the path forward on both weapons and human rights; and the third is to bring North Korea back to the table in order to contend with this very difficult problem.

North Korean Threat

We must first recognize that North Korea remains one of the greatest threats to the security of the American homeland today. It also continues to be the greatest proliferation threat in the world today, more so than Syria, and more so than Iran. Which begs the question, why have we not done more to stop this?

This administration's policy of "strategic patience" for the past seven years had placed this problem on the back burner. In the administration's own words, this policy was meant to accomplish two objectives in rolling back the North's programs. First, the United States would seek to break the cycle of provocations-for-negotiations that was the flaw of past administrations' policies by not reacting to every action by the North. Second, the consistent application of pressure would create a situation where Pyongyang would eventually feel compelled to return to the negotiating table genuinely motivated to uphold its denuclearization commitments. While the administration did make genuine efforts to engage with North Korea, these offers were rejected by the regime.

In the meantime, Kim Jong-un has been diligently improving his regime's capabilities over the course of this policy's application to disrupt and ultimately alter the strategic balance on the peninsula and in the region while our attention was directed elsewhere. But the issue should have been on the front-burner from day one, even if choices had to be made between options that were bad, and options that were worse. This problem cannot be punted to another administration, yet with just a year left, it is unlikely that the current administration has the capacity to engineer a breakthrough. Unfortunately strategic patience" turned to "benign neglect," and allowed space for North Korea to make technological progress in their programs unhindered. There have been four nuclear tests; three of them in the Obama administration; and two of them in the days preceding the President's State of the Union Speech.

My main concern is that North Korea does not fully comprehend the consequences of their drive to become a modern nuclear weapons state. It is not clear to me that they understand that nuclear weapons' value is in their strategic non-use. It is also probable that the young and inexperienced leader will make miscalculations because of his inflated and ill-informed view of the deterrent strength of these weapons to keep the United States and allies at bay. If the day ever comes when Kim Jong-un miscalculates the capability of his nuclear weapons stockpile, or his ever-improving long-range delivery capability, there will be no doubt horrible consequences for everyone. Then the whole world will wonder why regional powers – especially the U.S. – did not stop them before it was too late. We must not let that happen.

Therefore, we must first recognize that North Korea remains an ever-present threat to our nation's security and prosperity. Despite downsizing of conventional military capabilities in recent years to allocate more resources to its pursuit of nuclear weapons and to improve its asymmetric capability, the North Korean regime is still backed by a loyal army comprised of about 1.2 million active duty military personnel and 600,000 reservists, and possibly the largest number of Special Forces in the world.[1] According to the Department of Defense, approximately 70% of North Korea's ground forces and 50% of its air and naval forces are deployed within 100 kilometers of the de-militarized zone (DMZ), a tremendous threat not only to our troops stationed on the other side of the border, but also to the citizens of our trusted ally, South Korea.

Furthermore, open-source reporting on North Korea's ballistic missile program also reveals some troubling numbers; an estimated 700 SRBMs (capable of reaching South Korea), some 200 Nodong MRBMs (capable of reaching Japan), about 100 Musudan IRBMs, the potential successful development of ASCM and SLBM technologies (subject of two flight tests in May

---

[1] *The Military Balance 2015*, International Institute for Strategic Studies, p. 261.

and November 2015) and two types of ICBMs[2], the Taepodong-2 and the untested road-mobile KN-08, the latter which was subject of much speculation in 2015 when senior Department of Defense officials admitted to its potential completion.[3]

North Korea's growing cyber capabilities are something that we should pay more attention to. The November 2014 Sony incident finally brought this new threat to the consciousness of American policymakers and of the public. Our CSIS study completed last September found that the North is developing its cyber capabilities in tandem with its other asymmetric threats, and has embedded them within the very same party and military institutions that were responsible for provocative acts like the 2010 *Cheonan* sinking.[4] In the future, cyber-attacks could well be an integral part of a North Korean military strategy designed to disrupt and weaken U.S. military systems.

The 4th nuclear test last Wednesday reiterated that the threat from North Korea's nuclear program and growing asymmetric capabilities is very real. There is no comfort to be taken in scientists' skepticism of whether the hydrogen nuclear test succeeded. The test still had a yield more powerful than the previous three tests, which indicates technological progress in the nuclear program despite the sanctions regime. It is only a matter of time before they succeed.

Kim Jong-un must be made to understand the "non-utility" of his nuclear arsenal and that any such use would ultimately lead to his regime's final destruction. The one lesson from the nuclear revolution is that states with nuclear weapons do not use them. But whether the Kim regime understands the fundamentals of nuclear deterrence is questionable, and therefore remains a cause of tremendous concern. He must also understand the dangerous pathologies of being a nascent nuclear state. There will be temptation to transfer weapons, fissile material, or this technology to other states or terrorist groups to gain the foreign currencies his regime needs. His regime already has a history of selling its weapons systems.

So how do we "educate" the North of those pathologies of being a nuclear state? A better approach.

A New Approach – Asymmetric Pressure Points

A new approach to North Korea must focus on asymmetric pressure points. Two cases in recent history outline the effectiveness of such strategy, first was the September 2005 Banco Delta Asia (BDA) case where the Treasury Department undertook actions that led to the freezing of the assets of North Korean bank accounts in Macao. The second was the United Nations Commission of Inquiry report on North Korean human rights released in February 2014, which unequivocally called on the UN Security Council to refer the North's leadership to the International Criminal Court for a laundry list of crimes against humanity. Just a month

---

[2] SRBM stands for a short-range ballistic missile, MRBM for a medium-range ballistic missile, IRBM for an intermediate-range ballistic missile, ASCM for an anti-ship missile, SLBM for a submarine-launched ballistic missile, and ICBM for an intercontinental ballistic missile.

[3] Department of Defense Press Briefing by Admiral Gortney in the Pentagon Briefing Room, April 7, 2015. http://www.defense.gov/News/News-Transcripts/Transcript-View/Article/607034

[4] An executive summary of the CSIS cyber team report can be found here - Victor Cha, James Lewis, et al "Executive Summary: North Korea's Cyber Operations: Strategy and Responses," November 2015. http://csis.org/publication/executive-summary-north-koreas-cyber-operations-strategy-and-responses

ago the UN Security Council held the second meeting on human rights in North Korea, despite attempts again by the Chinese and the Russians to remove it from the agenda. And in both of those cases, the Kim regime – whether the father or the son – were truly frazzled, and completely caught off guard by outside actions. A strategy that creates costs for continued North Korean bad behavior and that affects a change in their direction must build on these pressure points.

Sanctions: The sanctions against North Korea pale in comparison to the level of sanctioning against Iran. Although there are 4 UNSCRs each directed at both Iran and North Korea, there are only 6 presidential executive orders for North Korea, while there are 17 for Iran. The number of individuals and entities sanctioned by the U.S. and UN are vastly disparate as well, 843 (U.S.) and 121 (UN) for Iran, but only 100 (U.S.) and 31 (UN) for North Korea (more information on these numbers are found in Appendix A). A new sanctions portfolio must fully exercise the authorities created in Presidential Executive Order 13687 – in response to the November 2014 Sony hack – to target additional individuals or entities for proliferation, human rights abuses and cyber-related activities. The E.O. was an innovation in that it was deliberately broad in scope to allow Treasury and U.S. law enforcement agencies to go after a range of behavior. Why it has not been used more fully to this point is puzzling.

Secondary sanctioning has been discussed in the policy community for some time as a significant escalation of the sanctions regime. This should be given positive consideration now to include third-party entities and individuals that facilitate North Korea's illegal and illicit activities. This will certainly complicate our relationships with China, the European Union, and countries in Southeast Asia, South America or Africa, but it is also certain that these entities will comply when given the choice between dealing with the North or with losing access to U.S. financial institutions.

Third, trade and commodity sanctions should be expanded to include sanctions of rare-earth minerals, coal and steel or goods like timber and agricultural products that are exported to other countries to earn foreign currencies for the North Korean regime. Expert estimates put rare earth minerals and steel exports at around $1.8 billion and $245 million respectively.[5] Again, this will complicate things for China, but the single most important causal factor for the growth of cash and a more stable economy in Pyongyang have been the extractive industry contracts signed between China and North Korea in 2008.

The U.S. government can work with the UN and countries in Northeast Asia to target and enhance sanctions enforcement against ports, shipping companies, and airline carriers that facilitate North Korea's illegal activities such as bulk cash smuggling and arms shipments. The U.S. can strengthen efforts to sanction these third party entities under the current regime or create additional measures that would prohibit ships flying North Korean flags or North Korean air carriers from accessing certain ports and airports around the world.

---

[5] Korea Trade Investment Promotion Agency (KOTRA), "Trends in 2013 North Korean Trade," July 2014, accessible here
http://www.globalwindow.org/gw/publishdata/GWPDIN020M.html?BBS_ID=30&MENU_CD=M10503&UPPE
R_MENU_CD=M10501&MENU_STEP=2&ARTICLE_ID=5018281

Primary Money Laundering Concern & State Sponsor of Terrorism: The U.S. should give serious consideration to designating North Korea or banks that do illicit business with North Korea as a jurisdiction or institution of primary money laundering concern. This was the key to the set of actions that led to freezing of North Korean assets in the 2005 BDA case. This would have a similar effect to imposing secondary sanctions on third party banks that facilitate North Korea's illegal activities.

U.S. officials should also give serious consideration to putting North Korea back on the State Sponsor of Terrorism list. State Department lawyers may disagree citing legal criteria, but the cyber actions against both South Korea and the United States in particular should be investigated as grounds for relisting. These cyber-attacks were ill-advisedly characterized by the administration as "criminal" acts but CSIS research shows these activities as instigated by the same entities in North Korea responsible for military aggression and terrorist acts.

Slave Labor: Human rights must complement sanctions as part of this asymmetric strategy. One of the potential targets would be North Korean slave labor. According to Marzuki Darusman, the UN special rapporteur on human rights in North Korea in October 2015, the regime has forced more than 50,000 people to work abroad in mining, logging, textile and the construction industries. These forced laborers are sent to places in Africa, Europe, the Middle East and Southeast Asia, but especially to Russia and China.[6] They are sent abroad with the sole rationale of circumventing sanctions and earning the regime currencies it sorely needs. Lower estimates put the number at about $150 – 250 million, but higher estimates put it between $1.5 – 2.5 billion annually. That is a substantial amount of money that we have reasonable cause to believe goes into bankrolling the North's nuclear and missile programs. This is an asymmetric pressure point that the international community and UN can, and must target. We have to call out, and pressure these countries, including China and Russia, to enforce ILO standards for the North Korean workers in host countries or to stop accepting them.

Kaesong Industrial Complex: Another useful asymmetric pressure point is the Kaesong Industrial Complex. A legacy of the sunshine policy, this project now provides $90 million in annual wages (around $245.7 million from December 2004 to July 2012) of hard currency to North Korean authorities with little wages actually going to the factory workers.[7] The South Korean government will be opposed to shutting this down, as even conservative governments in South Korea have grown attached to the project as symbolic of the future potential of a united Korea, but difficult times call for difficult measures.

Information: North Korea, under a young and insecure leadership, is hyper-sensitive to external criticism that hits at the heart of the regime's legitimacy and shatters the myth of its benign care of the Korean people. Nowhere has this been more apparent than in Pyongyang's

---

[6] "UN investigator: North Koreans doing forced labor abroad to earn foreign currency for country," *Associated Press*, October 28.
www.usnews.com/news/world/articles/2015/10/28/un-investigator-north-koreans-doing-forced-labor-abroad
[7] These numbers were cited in Yang Moon-soo, "Kaesong Industrial Complex as Key to Peace on Korean Peninsula," *Korea Focus*, 2013, available at
http://www.koreafocus.or.kr/design2/layout/content_print.asp?group_id=104914
Cumulative numbers for 2004 – July 2012 were cited in this *Chosun Ilbo* article here (In Korean)
http://news.chosun.com/site/data/html_dir/2012/10/08/2012100800446.html?Dep0=twitter&d=2012100800446

reaction to the screening of the movie *The Interview*, and its mad diplomatic scramble in response to the UN Commission of Inquiry recommendations for the regime to be referred to the ICC for crimes against humanity. In this regard, leader Kim is probably more incensed about the restart of loudspeaker broadcasts across the DMZ last Friday than he is about U.S. dispatching of a B-52 bomber to the peninsula over the weekend. With renewal of the North Korean Human Rights Act coming onto Congress's agenda, it would be prudent to increase both funding and means of information dissemination into North Korea. As I have argued before, the U.S. and South Korea should create a comprehensive strategy for breaking down North Korea's information barriers to reach a population with an insatiable thirst for news about the outside world.[8]

Diplomacy: The most useful diplomatic action at this point is not to put another deal on the table for the North. The Clinton and Bush presidencies did this. And the current administration, as evidenced by its outreach to Cuba, Myanmar, and Iran, has not been averse to putting packages in front of isolated regimes. Indeed, more than a couple of packages of proposals have already been put before Pyongyang by this administration. The problem is that North Korea is not interested in talking.

The five members of the Six-Party Talks, China, Japan, South Korea, Russia and the U.S. should convene to discuss steps forward and potential contingencies. The five parties should confirm the 2005 Six Party Joint Statement as the only written document in which the North has pledged in writing "to abandon all nuclear weapons and existing nuclear programs." It is important for the UN also to reaffirm the validity of this document and North Korea's pledge as a political response to Kim's actions. They have to be prepared for North Korean responses to new sanctions. We need to have a more open discussion about the future of the Korean Peninsula and unification.

The region: A new U.S. approach cannot realistically bank on China abandoning the Pyongyang regime or cutting off all energy shipments, as dissatisfied as Beijing may be with Kim's behavior. Indeed, the U.S. should not want to entirely subcontract this vital national security issue to its principal competitor in the Asia-Pacific. But the U.S. can push for Beijing to titrate its sustenance to the regime. China could first undertake an internal audit of all private and state-owned companies doing business on the Sino-North Korean border to understand the scope of the problem. At the official level, it can commit not to cease all ongoing economic projects and reject calls for any new ones until the regime returns to negotiations. Beijing could commit to abstain from (i.e., not obstruct) any UN Security Council discussions on human rights abuses in the North. But none of this would be remotely possible until Washington frames the North Korea issue (not just climate change) as a major metric of cooperation in US-China relations.

The nuclear test last week also underlines the need for the United States to be able to coordinate seamlessly with its two key allies, Japan and South Korea. Improving the ability of the three to share intelligence is critical and agreements to this effect need to be forged. Though South Korea has expressed reluctance in the past, it is necessary to have a discussion

---

[8] Victor Cha, "Light Through the Darkness," The Bush Institute at George W. Bush Presidential Center, January 2015, available at http://www.bushcenter.org/sites/default/files/gwb_north_korea_report_call_to_action.pdf

Cha: North Korea Testimony to HFAC Subcommittee on Asia   January 13, 2016 8

about better missile defense cooperation, including the emplacement of THAAD on the peninsula.

If implemented correctly, such a strategy could strangle the regime. But it could also show the North that their weapons are unusable and that the only exit is a process of negotiation in which all issues, including security, human rights, and economics, are addressed.

Appendix A: Comparison of Sanctions on Iran and North Korea

	Iran	North Korea
*U.S. Executive Orders**	17	6
*U.S. Sanctions Listed Entities & Individuals**	843	100
UNSC Resolutions (imposing sanctions)	4	4
*UN Sanctions Listed Entities & Individuals** *(as of 2013)*	78 entities & 43 individuals	19 entities & 12 individuals

*U.S. numbers are drawn from the OneFreeKorea blog, the Department of Treasury, Office of Foreign Assets Control's Specially Designated Nationals List for North Korea and Iran, and the Congressional Research Service, while the UN numbers are drawn from the UN Special Research Report on UN Sanctions (2013).

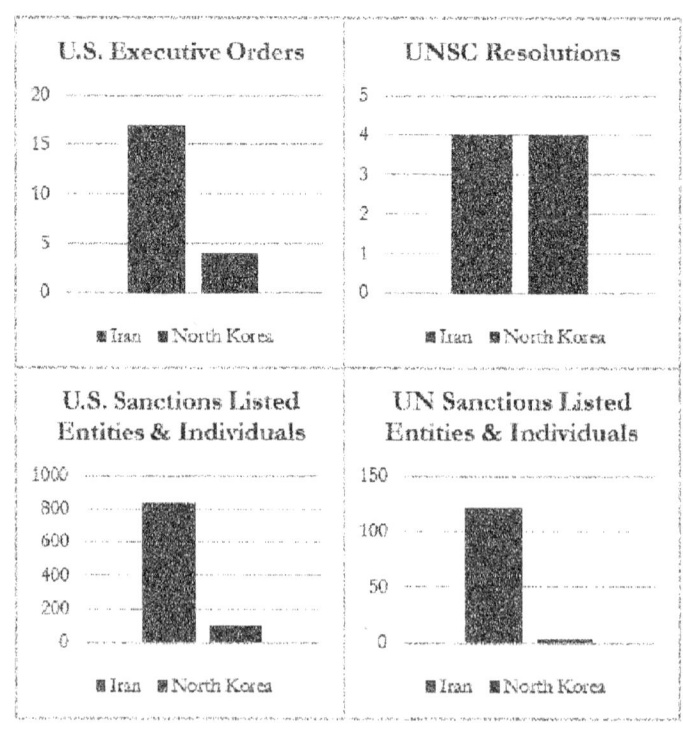

Mr. SALMON. Thank you.

Mr. Klingner.

STATEMENT OF MR. BRUCE KLINGNER, SENIOR RESEARCH FELLOW FOR NORTHEAST ASIA, THE HERITAGE FOUNDATION

Mr. KLINGNER. Thank you, Mr. Chairman, Ranking Member Sherman, and other distinguished members of the panel. It truly is an honor to be asked to appear before you on such an important issue to our national security.

North Korea's recent nuclear test has again triggered widespread calls to do something tougher on North Korea. But we have been here many times before, and each time administration claims of tough action were taken at face value, pledges to be even tougher the next time were issued, and interest was eventually diverted elsewhere.

More effective action was also hindered by several widely accepted myths about North Korean sanctions. The first myth is that sanctions can't affect an isolated country like North Korea. Targeted financial measures, which are a law enforcement mechanism, are directed against specific entities that violate U.S. laws. Even the most isolated regime, criminal organization, or terrorist group is tied into the global financial order.

The vast majority of all international financial transactions, including those of North Korea, are denominated in dollars, which means they must go through a U.S. Treasury Department regulated bank in the United States. That gives the United States tremendous power and leverage to freeze and seize assets, to impose fines such as a $9-billion fine imposed on a French bank for improper financial transactions with Cuba, Iran, and Sudan, and also to deny access to the U.S. financial system.

As you already pointed out, Mr. Chairman, a second myth is that North Korea is the most heavily sanctioned country in the world. President Obama claims North Korea is the most isolated, the most sanctioned, the most cutoff nation on Earth. That is simply not true. The U.S., the European Union, and the U.N. imposed far more pervasive and compelling measures against Iran than North Korea.

Also, unilaterally, the United States has targeted far fewer North Korean entities than those of the Balkans, Burma, Cuba, Iran, and Zimbabwe. The U.S. has sanctioned more than twice as many Zimbabwean entities as North Korean entities. We have also designated Iran and Burma as primary money laundering concerns, but not North Korea, which is counterfeiting our currency.

The U.S. has sanctioned officials from Burma, Burundi, Congo, Iran, Syria, Sudan, and Zimbabwe, for human rights violations, and sanctioned by name the Presidents of Belarus and Zimbabwe, but not yet sanctioned a single North Korean entity for human rights violations nearly 2 years after a U.N. Commission of Inquiry report concluded the regime was conducting such egregious human rights violations as to constitute crimes against humanity.

The U.S. has also frozen the assets of Sudan, Iranian, and Syrian, but not North Korean, officials and entities for censorship. The list goes on and on, and I have included other examples in my written testimony.

A third myth is there is nothing more the U.S. can impose on North Korea. After he left office, former Assistant Secretary of State Kurt Campbell commented, "It would be possible for us to put more financial pressure on North Korea. We can make life much more difficult through financial sanctions on North Korea." And he also pointed out he was surprised when he was in government to find out that there were about 10 times as many sanctions on Burma as there were on North Korea.

President Obama, Secretary of State John Kerry, and other officials have made similar statements indicating that there are other measures that the U.S. could impose but hasn't.

A fourth myth is that sanctions don't work. As Dr. Cha already pointed out, tougher measures were effective when applied. In 2005, the U.S. designated the Macao-based bank Banco Delta Asia as a money laundering concern for facilitating North Korean illicit activities. As a result of Washington belatedly enforcing its laws, as well as a series of sub rosa meetings by U.S. officials throughout Asia, two dozen financial institutions voluntarily cut back or terminated their business with North Korea.

And a North Korea negotiator admitted to a senior White House official, "You finally found a way to hurt us." Instead, what the U.S. should be doing is implementing the Iran model against North Korea. Just as strong international measures induced Tehran back to the negotiating table, more robust measures are needed to leverage North Korea.

While implementing new sanctions measures is important, fully implementing and enforcing already existing, far-reaching measures is also critical. The U.S. has the tools; we have just lacked the resolve to fully use them.

For years the Obama administration has been hitting the snooze bar on sanctions. It has pursued a policy of timid incrementalism by holding some sanctions in abeyance to be rolled out after the next North Korean violation or provocation. The U.S. instead needs to sharpen the choices for North Korea by raising the risk and cost for those violating laws and U.N. resolutions, not only North Korea but also those that facilitate its actions.

In my written testimony, I provided a lengthy list of very specific recommendations for U.S. and South Korean actions that should be implemented against North Korea. Neither sanctions nor diplomacy alone is a panacea. Both are essential and, along with fully funding U.S. defense requirements, should be mutually reinforcing elements of a comprehensive integrated strategy.

I will conclude my presentation with the same question I posed to this committee 2 years ago. Why has the United States hesitated to impose the same legal measures against North Korea that it has already used against other countries for far less egregious violations of U.S. and international law?

Thank you again for the privilege of appearing before you.

[The prepared statement of Mr. Klingner follows:]

The Heritage Foundation
LEADERSHIP FOR AMERICA

214 Massachusetts Avenue, NE • Washington DC 20002 • (202) 546-4400 • heritage.org

CONGRESSIONAL TESTIMONY

Moving Beyond Timid Incrementalism: Time to Fully Implement U.S. Laws on North Korea

Testimony before
Subcommittee on Asia and the Pacific of the Foreign Affairs Committee
United States House of Representatives

"The U.S. Response to North Korea's Nuclear Provocations"

January 13, 2016

Bruce Klingner
Senior Research Fellow, Northeast Asia
The Heritage Foundation

Moving Beyond Timid Incrementalism:
Time to Fully Implement U.S. Laws on North Korea
Bruce Klingner

My name is Bruce Klingner. I am the Senior Research Fellow for Northeast Asia at The Heritage Foundation. The views I express in this testimony are my own, and should not be construed as representing any official position of The Heritage Foundation.

North Korean Nuclear Threat

North Korea announced on January 4 that it had conducted a successful H-bomb nuclear test of a miniaturized warhead. Nuclear experts continue to analyze the data, but preliminary assessments are that North Korea did indeed conduct its fourth nuclear test, though it is more likely that Pyongyang has achieved a boosted fission rather than a fusion bomb. Such a weapon would be larger than Pyongyang's first three nuclear tests (and the 1945 U.S. atomic weapons), but not of the magnitude of a hydrogen fusion bomb.

If confirmed, North Korea's fourth nuclear test, particularly of an improved weapon, is a dangerous development. With its ongoing development of several different missile systems, North Korea poses an increasing direct threat to the United States, South Korea, and Japan. Experts estimate that Pyongyang currently has 10–16 nuclear weapons, with the potential to increase that cache to as many as 50–100 by 2020.[1]

North Korea has likely already achieved warhead miniaturization, the ability to place nuclear weapons on its medium-range missiles, and a preliminary ability to reach the continental U.S. with a missile.[2] The regime's No Dong medium-range ballistic missiles put Japan and parts of South Korea under a nuclear threat today. North Korea also continues its development of long-range missiles to attack the United States.

In April 2013, U.S. officials told reporters that North Korea "can put a nuclear weapon on a missile, that they have missile-deliverable nuclear weapons, but not ones that can go more than 1,000 miles."[3] In October 2014, General Curtis M. Scaparrotti, senior U.S. commander on the Korean Peninsula, told reporters that North Korea has the ability to produce a miniaturized nuclear warhead that can be mounted on a ballistic missile.[4]

U.S. experts concluded that the North Korean missile recovered from the ocean floor by the South Korean navy after the December 2012 launch provided "tangible proof that North Korea was building the missile's cone at dimensions for a nuclear warhead, durable enough to be

---

[1] Joel S. Wit and Sun Young Ahn, "North Korea's Nuclear Futures: Technology and Strategy," Johns Hopkins University, U.S.–Korea Institute at SAIS, February 2015, http://38north.org/wp-content/uploads/2015/02/NKNF-NK-Nuclear-Futures-Wit-0215.pdf (accessed January 11, 2016).

[2] Bruce Klingner, "Allies Should Confront Imminent North Korean Nuclear Threat," Heritage Foundation *Backgrounder* No. 2913, June 3, 2014, http://www.heritage.org/research/reports/2014/06/allies-should-confront-imminent-north-korean-nuclear-threat.

[3] NBC News, "Will North Korea Follow Through on Nuclear Threats?" *Nightly News*, April 3, 2013, http://www.nbcnews.com/video/nightly-news/51421978 (accessed January 11, 2016).

[4] General Curtis Scaparrotti and Rear Admiral John Kirby, "Department of Defense Press Briefing by General Scaparrotti in the Pentagon Briefing Room," transcript, October 24, 2014, http://www.defense.gov/Transcripts/Transcript.aspx?Transcriptid=5525 (accessed January 11, 2016).

placed on a long-range missile that could re-enter the earth's atmosphere from space." A U.S. official added that South Korea provided other intelligence suggesting that North Korea had "mastered the miniaturization and warhead design as well."[5] In March 2013, Minister of Defense Kim Kwan-jin told the National Assembly that the missile had a range of more than 10,000 kilometers (km) and could have reached the U.S. West Coast.[6] New York and Washington, DC, are approximately 11,000 km from North Korea.

In April 2015, Admiral Bill Gortney, commander of North American Aerospace Defense Command (NORAD), told reporters that the KN-08 road-mobile intercontinental ballistic missile (ICBM) "is operational today. Our assessment is that they have the ability to put a nuclear weapon on a KN-08 and shoot it at the [U.S.] homeland." The four-star commanders of U.S. Forces Korea and Pacific Command have made similar threat assessments.[7]

According to The Heritage Foundation's calculations, North Korea's Taepo Dong 2 missiles, with a range of 10,000 kilometers, are within strike capability of 120.6 million people, or 38 percent of the U.S. population.

North Korean missiles can reach U.S.

With a range of 10,000 kilometers, North Korea's Taepo Dong 2 missile can reach most of the continental U.S. About **120.6 million people** live in those areas, or 38 percent of the U.S. population.

Source: Heritage Foundation calculations using data from the U.S. Census Bureau.   heritage.org

---

[5]Eli Lake, "US Recovery of North Korean Satellite Exposed Nuclear Progress," *The Telegraph*, April 15, 2013, http://www.telegraph.co.uk/journalists/the-daily-beast/9995514/US-recovery-of-North-Korean-satellite-exposed-nuclear-progress.html (accessed January 11, 2016).

[6]"S. Korea Says Debris Reveals North's ICBM Technology," Voice of America, December 23, 2012. http://www.voanews.com/content/north-korea-missile/1570703.html (accessed January 11, 2016), and "N. Korea Rocket 'Could Fly 10,000 km,'" *The Chosun Ilbo*, April 16, 2012, http://english.chosun.com/site/data/html_dir/2012/04/16/2012041601302.html (accessed January 11, 2016)..

[7]Zachary Keck, "Assessing the North Korea Nuclear Threat," *The Diplomat*, May 1, 2015, http://thediplomat.com/2015/05/assessing-the-north-korea-nuclear-threat/ (accessed January 11, 2016).

North Korean Cyber Threat

The United States assessed that North Korea was responsible for the cyber attack against Sony Pictures in 2014. Contrary to the perception that North Korea is a technically backward nation, the regime has an active cyber warfare capability. The Reconnaissance General Bureau has 3,000 "cyber-warriors" dedicated to attacking Pyongyang's enemies.[8] Seoul concluded that North Korea was behind cyber attacks against South Korean government agencies, businesses, banks, and media organizations in 2009, 2011, 2012, and 2013. A South Korean cyber expert assessed that North Korea's electronic warfare capabilities were surpassed only by the United States and Russia.[9]

President Obama denounced the attack against Sony Pictures and issued Executive Order 13687. According to Assistant Secretary of Treasury Daniel Glaser, the executive order is a "significant broadening of Treasury's authority to increase pressure" on North Korea since the U.S. for the first time can designate entities "solely on their status as officials or agencies" of the North Korean government.[10]

Because the executive order provides for *affiliation*-based rather than *conduct*-based sanctions, the U.S. does not need to disclose as much detailed evidentiary information, including potentially sensitive intelligence data, when putting an entity or organization on the sanctions list.

U.S. Response Weakly Implemented. The executive order, though expansive in legal breadth, was only weakly implemented by the Obama Administration. The U.S. targeted 13 North Korean entities, three organizations already on the U.S. sanctions list, and 10 individuals not involved in cyber warfare. Although White House officials described the executive order as "a first step…this is certainly not the end," the Administration has not followed up with any additional measures a year later. Nor were any North Korean entities sanctioned under the Obama Administration's April 2015 cyber executive order.[11]

North Korea as a Terrorist Nation

North Korea's cyber attack and accompanying threats of a "9/11-type attack" appear to fulfill the legal definition of international terrorism. Under various statutes of U.S. law (the most relevant being 18 U.S. Code § 2331), international terrorism is defined as acts that:
> (A) involve violent acts or acts dangerous to human life that are a violation of the criminal laws of the United States or of any State, or that would be a criminal violation if committed within the jurisdiction of the United States or of any State;
> (B) appear to be intended—

---

[8] Sangwon Yoon, "North Korea Recruits Hackers at School," Al-Jazeera, June 20, 2011, http://www.aljazeera.com/indepth/features/2011/06/201162081543573839.html (accessed January 11, 2016).
[9] "N. Korea Boosting Cyber Warfare Capabilities," *The Chosun Ilbo*, November 5, 2013, http://english.chosun.com/site/data/html_dir/2013/11/05/2013110501790.html (accessed January 11, 2016).
[10] "Testimony of Assistant Secretary Daniel L. Glaser before the House Foreign Affairs Committee Confronting North Korea's Cyber Threat, January 13, 2015, https://www.treasury.gov/press-center/press-releases/Pages/jl9738.aspx (accessed January 12, 2016.
[11] "Executive Order – 'Blocking the Property of Certain Persons Engaging in Significant Malicious Cyber-Enabled Activities,'" The White House, April 1, 2015, https://www.whitehouse.gov/the-press-office/2015/04/01/executive-order-blocking-property-certain-persons-engaging-significant-m (accessed January 11, 2016).

> (i) to intimidate or coerce a civilian population;
> (ii) to influence the policy of a government by intimidation or coercion; or
> (iii) to affect the conduct of a government by mass destruction, assassination, or kidnapping; and would be a criminal violation if committed within the jurisdiction of the United States and are intended to intimidate or coerce a civilian population.[12]

As such, the United States should return North Korea to the state sponsors of terrorism list. Pyongyang had been on the list until the Bush Administration removed it in 2008 in a failed attempt to stimulate progress in the Six-Party Talks nuclear negotiations.

In addition to the threats of violence following the Sony hack, North Korea has provided support for other acts of international terrorism since its removal from the terrorist list. These acts include:[13]

- Seoul concluded that North Korea was behind cyber attacks using viruses or distributed denial-of-service tactics against South Korean government agencies, businesses, banks, and media organizations in 2009, 2011, 2012, and 2013.
- In June 2012, Seoul Metropolitan Police arrested a South Korean man for violating the National Security Law. The man had met in China with North Korean agents of the General Reconnaissance Bureau to purchase software with malignant viruses which were used to conduct a cyber attack on Incheon International Airport.[14]
- In May 2012, North Korea jammed GPS signals affecting hundreds of civilian airliners flying in and out of South Korea. The Korea Communications Commission stated the signals came from Kaesong in North Korea.[15]
- In April 2012, North Korean agent An Hak-young was sentenced to four years' imprisonment by a South Korean court for plotting to assassinate outspoken anti-Pyongyang activist Park Sang-hak with a poison-tipped needle.[16]
- In July 2010, two agents of the North Korean ruling party's General Reconnaissance Bureau were arrested by South Korean authorities and pled guilty before a South Korean court to attempting to assassinate high-level defector Hwang Jang-Yop who was residing in South Korea. Kim Myung-ho and Do Myung-kwan were sentenced to 10 years in jail.[17] Kim admitted to being an agent of the North Korean General Reconnaissance Bureau and ordered to assassinate Hwang.

---

[12] 18 U.S. Code § 2331 – Definitions, Cornell University Law School, http://www.law.cornell.edu/uscode/text/18/2331 (accessed January 11, 2016).

[13] For a more in-depth analysis, see Joshua Stanton, *Arsenal of Terror: North Korea State Sponsor of Terrorism* (The Committee for Human Rights in North Korea, 2015).

[14] "Incheon Airport Cyberattack Traced to Pyongyang," *Joongang Daily*, June 5, 2012.

[15] "N.Korea's GPS Jamming is Terrorism Pure and Simple," *The Chosun Ilbo*, May 11, 2012.

[16] Park Chan-Kyong, "Seoul Arrests Suspected N. Korean Assassin," AFP, September 15, 2011, and Ashley Rowland, "South Korea Court Upholds Prison Term for Would-Be Assassin," *Stars and Stripes*, November 29, 2012.

[17] Chris Green, "Assassins Get Ten Years for Hwang Plot," The Daily NK, July 1, 2010, and Mok Young-jae, "Prosecution Requests 15 Years for Hwang Assassins," The Daily NK, June 23, 2010.

- In 2009, three shipments of North Korean conventional arms were seized. Western and Israeli intelligence officials believe the shipments were bound for Hamas and Hezbollah.[18]
    - In July, an Australian-owned ship was seized in the United Arab Emirates carrying North Korean weapons bound for Iran. The ship contained banned North Korean weapons, including rocket-propelled grenades, headed for Iran on the Australian-owned, Bahamas-flagged cargo ship ANL Australia.[19]
    - In November, the Israeli Navy intercepted a large arms consignment (500 tons) shipped by Iran to Syria on the vessel Francop. Some of the shipment (122mm rocket parts) appear to have originated in North Korea.[20]
    - In December, Thai authorities seized 35 tons of North Korean weapons, including rockets and rocket-propelled grenades that were determined to be enroute to terrorist groups Hamas and Hezbollah.[21]
- October 2008, a North Korea woman was convicted by a South Korean court as a spy and plotting to kill South Korean intelligence agents with poisoned needles.[22]

North Korea Commits "Crimes Against Humanity"

In February 2013, a United Nations Commission of Inquiry report provided a chilling litany of horrors that the North Korean regime had inflicted upon its citizens. The commission issued a damning condemnation of the North Korea government for "systemic, widespread, and gross violations of human rights" that were of such a monumental scale as to constitute "crimes against humanity." It also advocated adopting targeted sanctions against those most responsible for these crimes against humanity.

Secretary of State John Kerry rightfully described North Korea's human rights abuses as "horrific [and] one of the most egregious examples of reckless disregard for human rights and for human beings anywhere on the planet." He called for the international community to continue to "shed light on North Korea's atrocities against its own people [and] ramp up international pressure."

---

[18]Joby Warrick, "Arms Smuggling Heightens Iran Fears," *The Washington Post*, December 3, 2009, p. A14, and "Iran Bought Masses of N Korean Arms," *The Chosun Ilbo Online*, December 4, 2009.

[19]"Australia Investigates Seizure of Ship in UAE with North Korean Weapons Going to Iran," Associated Press, August 30, 2009, http://www.nydailynews.com/news/world/australia-investigates-seizure-ship-uae-north-korean-weapons-iran-article-1.401152 (accessed January 11, 2016), and Peter Spiegel and Chip Cummins, "Cargo of North Korea Matériel Is Seized en Route to Iran," *The Wall Street Journal*, August 31, 2009, http://www.wsj.com/news/articles/SB125151138304468869 (accessed January 11, 2016).

[20]U.N. Panel of Experts Report, March 6, 2014, paragraph 108, http://www.un.org/ga/search/view_doc.asp?symbol=S/2014/147 (accessed January 11, 2016).

[21]"Thailand Seizes 'Arms Plane Flying from North Korea,'" BBC, December 12, 2009, http://news.bbc.co.uk/2/hi/asia-pacific/8410042.stm (accessed January 11, 2016); "Israel Says Seized North Korean Arms Were for Hamas, Hezbollah," Reuters, May 12, 2010; "Korean Arms Cache Caught En Route to Mideast," *Daily Star Online* (Beirut), December 15, 2009; and U.N. Panel of Experts report, June 11, 2013, http://www.un.org/ga/search/view_doc.asp?symbol=S/2013/337 (accessed January 11, 2016).

[22]"North Korean Spy Jailed in Sex-for-Secrets Case," NBC, October 15, 2008, http://www.nbcnews.com/id/27192149/ns/world_news-asia_pacific/t/north-korean-spy-jailed-sex-for-secrets-case/ (accessed January 11, 2016).

No U.S. Sanctions for Human Rights Violations. Yet, the Obama Administration has taken no action nearly two years after the U.N. Commission of Inquiry concluded in February 2014 that Pyongyang had committed human rights violations so egregious as to qualify as crimes against humanity. In March 2015, the Obama Administration expressed "deep concern," and in April 2015, the State Department vowed it was "reviewing options" over North Korean human rights violations. In December 2015, U.S. Ambassador to the U.N. vowed, "We are documenting your crimes, and one day you will be judged for them."[23]

To date, the United States has targeted zero—yes, zero—North Korean entities for human rights violations. By contrast, the U.S. has targeted Zimbabwe, Congo, and Burma for human rights violations. Washington sanctioned by name the presidents of Zimbabwe and Belarus but has yet to name Kim Jong-un or the heads of any of the North Korean organizations listed by the U.N. Commission of Inquiry report.

Sanctions: An Important and Variable Component of Foreign Policy
Sanctions[24] are punitive measures intended to deter, coerce, and compel changes in another country's policy and behavior. During the past decade, the U.S. government adopted a more effective financial strategy against rogue regimes. Washington now uses *targeted* financial measures against regimes and violators and not the citizens of a country.

An effective sanctions strategy is based on several key precepts:
1. Even the most isolated regime has to move its money across borders;
2. Because the U.S. dollar is the principal reserve and trading currency around the world, almost all international transactions are denominated in dollars which must go through the U.S. financial system; and
3. Financial institutions are driven to police themselves by aversion to reputational risk and exclusion from the U.S. financial system, which provides Washington with very strong leverage against rogue regimes.

Critics of coercive financial pressure question its effectiveness because they have not yet forced Pyongyang to abandon its nuclear and missile programs, but neither did repeated bilateral and multilateral negotiations or unconditional engagement. Adopting such a narrow viewpoint overlooks the multifaceted utility of sanctions, which:

1. **Show** resolve to enforce international agreements and send a strong signal to other nuclear aspirants. If laws are not enforced and defended, they cease to have value.
2. **Impose** a heavy penalty on violators to demonstrate that there are consequences for defying international agreements and transgressing the law.
3. **Constrain** North Korea's ability to acquire the components, technology, and finances to augment and expand its arsenal.
4. **Impede** North Korean nuclear, missile, and conventional arms proliferation. Targeted financial and regulatory measures increase both the risk and the operating costs of North Korea's continued violations of Security Council resolutions and international law.

---

[23]"Ambassador Power on Human Rights in North Korea," U.S. Mission to the U.N., December 11, 2015, http://usun.state.gov/highlights/7036 (accessed January 11, 2016).
[24]For the purposes of this paper, the terms *sanctions, targeted financial or regulatory measures,* and *coercive financial pressure* will be used interchangeably, although there are some technical differences among them.

5. In conjunction with other policy tools, **seek** to modify North Korean behavior.

Six Myths About North Korean Sanctions

Myth 1. The U.S. and other nations face a policy choice between sanctions or engagement. Sanctions and diplomatic engagement are most effective when integrated into a comprehensive strategy that engages all of the instruments of national power, including diplomatic, information, military, and economic. No tool is meant to be used in isolation. Not fully utilizing any element of national power reduces the effectiveness of U.S. foreign policy.

When debating the efficacy of sanctions, it is important to recognize that diplomatic engagement has failed to curtail North Korea's two nuclear programs. Pyongyang violated each of the four international agreements it signed to never pursue nuclear weapons programs. Four subsequent agreements to abandon the weapons it promised never to build also collapsed. Over a 20-year period, the international community has pursued two-party, three-party, four-party and six-party negotiations—all have failed.

Myth 2. Sanctions cannot affect an isolated country like North Korea. When people hear of sanctions, they usually think of trade sanctions, i.e., refusing to allow trade. But it also includes targeted financial measures which are directed against specific entities that violate U.S. laws. It exploits their need to access the global financial network. Even the most isolated regime, criminal organization, or terrorist group is tied to the global financial order. Dirty money eventually has to cross borders.

The vast majority of all international financial transactions are denominated in U.S. dollars. And every dollar-denominated transaction anywhere in the world must go through a U.S. Treasury Department–regulated bank in the United States. That means, money sent from Australia to London or from Macau to Pyongyang goes through New York.

This gives the U.S. government tremendous power and leverage. For banks and businesses, there are catastrophic risks to facilitating illicit transactions. A British bank was fined $2 billion for money-laundering and sanctions violations, including financial dealings with Iran, and a French bank was fined $9 billion for processing banned transactions with Sudan, Iran, and Cuba.

Beyond having to pay fines and having assets frozen or seized, financial institutions can be designated as a "money-laundering concern" and denied access to the U.S. financial system. Given the centrality of the U.S. financial system to the international system, that would be the kiss of death for any financial institution and it would be shunned by every other financial institution.

Myth 3. North Korea is the most heavily sanctioned country in the world.[25] President Obama claims North Korea "is the most isolated, the most sanctioned, the most cut-off nation on Earth." That is simply not true. The U.S., the European Union, and the U.N. imposed far more pervasive and compelling measures against Iran than North Korea. Unilaterally, the United States has:

---

[25]I am indebted to my colleague, Joshua Stanton, author of *Arsenal of Terror: North Korea, State Sponsor of Terrorism*, for many of these comparisons.

- Targeted far fewer North Korean entities than those of the Balkans, Burma, Cuba, Iran, and Zimbabwe. The U.S. has sanctioned more than twice as many Zimbabwean entities than it has North Korean entities.
- Designated Iran and Burma as primary money-laundering concerns under Section 311 of the Patriot Act, but not North Korea, which counterfeits our currency.
- Targeted Burma, Congo, and Zimbabwe for human rights violations, and sanctioned by name the presidents of Belarus and Zimbabwe, but not yet sanctioned a single North Korean entity for human rights violations even two years after the U.N. Commission of Inquiry declared Pyongyang had committed crimes against humanity.
- Frozen the assets of Syrian,[26] Iranian,[27] Sudanese,[28] and Burundian[29] (but not North Korean) officials for human rights violations.
- Designated Iran and Syria as state sponsors of terrorism, but not North Korea.
- Frozen the assets of Iranian[30] and Syrian[31] (but not North Korean) officials and entities for censorship, and fined the enablers of censorship in Sudan, Iran, and Syria (but not North Korea).[32]
- Frozen the assets of nearly all of the leaders of Belarus[33] and Zimbabwe[34] (but not North Korea) for undermining democratic processes or institutions.
- Sanctioned the Islamic Republic of Iran Broadcasting service and its director of news services for "censorship or other activities that limit the freedom of expression," but has not sanctioned the Korean Central News Agency, the Rodong Sinmun, or Korea Central Television.[35]

---

[26]Executive Order 13606. "Blocking the Property and Suspending Entry Into the United States of Certain Persons With Respect to Grave Human Rights Abuses by the Governments of Iran and Syria via Information Technology," April 22, 2012, https://www.treasury.gov/resource-center/sanctions/Programs/Documents/13606.pdf (accessed January 11, 2016).

[27]"Executive Order 13553-- Designating Iranian Officials Responsible for or Complicit in Serious Human Rights Abuses," September 29, 2010, https://www.whitehouse.gov/the-press-office/2010/09/29/executive-order-13553-designating-iranian-officials-responsible-or-compl (accessed January 11, 2016).

[28]"Executive Order 13412—Blocking Property and Prohibiting Transactions With the Government of Sudan," October 17, 2006, https://www.treasury.gov/resource-center/sanctions/documents/13412.pdf (accessed January 11, 2016).

[29]"Obama Sanctions Burundi (but not North Korea) for Human Rights Violations," One Free Korea, November 29. 2015, http://freekorea.us/2015/11/29/obama-sanctions-burundi-but-not-north-korea-for-human-rights-violations/ (accessed January 11, 2016).

[30]"Treasury Designates Iranian Ministry of Intelligence and Security for Human Rights Abuses and Support for Terrorism," February 16, 2012, https://www.treasury.gov/press-center/press-releases/Pages/tg1424.aspx (accessed January 11, 2016).

[31]Executive Order 13606, op. cit.

[32]"Obama Sanctions Syria's Russian Enablers (but not North Korea's Chinese Enablers)," One Free Korea, December 2, 2015. http://freekorea.us/2015/12/02/obama-sanctions-syrias-russian-enablers-but-not-north-koreas-chinese-enablers/ (accessed January 11, 2016).

[33]Executive Order, "Blocking Property of Certain Persons Undermining Democratic Processes or Institutions in Belarus." https://www.treasury.gov/resource-center/sanctions/Documents/belarus_eo.pdf (accessed January 11, 2016).

[34]"Executive Order 13288—Blocking Property of Persons Undermining Democratic Processes or Institutions in Zimbabwe," https://www.treasury.gov/resource-center/sanctions/Documents/13288.pdf (accessed January 11, 2016).

[35]"Obama Sanctions Enablers of Censorship in Iran, Sudan & Syria (but not North Korea)," One Free Korea, November 30, 2015, http://freekorea.us/2015/11/30/obama-sanctions-enablers-of-censorship-in-iran-sudan-syria-but-not-north-korea/ (accessed January 11. 2016).

- Sanctioned Burmese officials for buying arms from North Korea, but no senior North Korean officials for selling them.[36]
- In response to the Russian invasion of Ukraine, the U.S. sanctioned 16 people for being Russian officials[37] and froze the assets of Russian[38] (but not North Korean) officials and financiers for aggression against a neighboring country.

Myth 4. There is nothing more the U.S. can impose on North Korea. The U.S. has pursued a policy in which it incrementally increases punishments on Pyongyang for its repeated defiance of the international community. After he left office, former Assistant Secretary of State Kurt Campbell commented, "I thought North Korea was the most sanctioned country in the world, but I was (proven) wrong.... Myanmar is sanctioned about 10 times (more than) North Korea.... It would be possible for us to put more financial pressure on North Korea.... We can make life much more difficult through financial sanctions on North Korea."[39]

Other Obama Administration officials have acknowledged that there is far more that could be done. In 2009, the State Department's sanctions czar commented that the Administration was considering additional measures against North Korea. U.S. Six-Party Talks negotiator Glynn Davies said in 2013, "I think that there are always more sanctions we could put in place if needed."[40] In March 2013, despite North Korea's repeated violations of U.N. resolutions, a State Department official commented that there was still room to increase sanctions on North Korea: "[W]e haven't maxed out, there is headroom."[41]

President Barack Obama promised in 2013 a "significant, serious enforcement of sanctions."[42] In April 2014, President Obama declared the U.S. would consider "further sanctions that have even more bite."[43] Several years ago, a U.S. official privately commented that Washington was considering a "list of blood curdling sanctions."

In May 2015, Secretary of State Kerry declared international intent to "increase the pressure and

---

[36]"Executive Order 13619 Blocking Property of Persons Threatening the Peace, Security, or Stability of Burma," July 11, 2012, https://www.treasury.gov/resource-center/sanctions/Programs/Documents/13619.pdf (accessed January 11, 2016).

[37]News release, "Treasury Sanctions Russian Officials, Members of the Russian Leadership's Inner Circle, and an Entity for Involvement in the Situation in Ukraine," March 20, 2014, https://www.treasury.gov/press-center/press-releases/Pages/jl23331.aspx (accessed January 11, 2016).

[38]"Executive Order 13662—Blocking Property of Additional Persons Contributing to the Situation in Ukraine," March 24, 2014, https://www.treasury.gov/resource-center/sanctions/Programs/Documents/ukraine_eo3.pdf (accessed January 11, 2016).

[39]"U.S. Needs to Toughen Sanctions on Recalcitrant N. Korea: Campbell," Yonhap, September 26, 2014.

[40]Glyn Davies, Special Representative for North Korea Policy, "Remarks to Press at Ministry of Foreign Affairs," Tokyo, Japan, November 25, 2013, http://www.state.gov/p/eap/rls/rm/2013/11/218034.htm (accessed January 11, 2016).

[41]Adrian Croft, "U.S. Wants EU to Put North Korean Bank on Sanctions List," Reuters, March 25, 2013, http://www.reuters.com/article/2013/03/25/us-korea-north-eu-idUSBRE92O0TU20130325 (accessed January 11, 2016).

[42]"Remarks by President Obama and President Lee of the Republic of Korea in Joint Press Availability," The White House, June 16, 2009, https://www.whitehouse.gov/the-press-office/remarks-president-obama-and-president-lee-republic-korea-joint-press-availability (accessed January 11, 2016).

[43]"President Obama Holds a Press Conference with President Park of the Republic of Korea," April 25, 2014, The White House, https://www.whitehouse.gov/photos-and-video/video/2014/04/25/president-obama-s-holds-press-conference-president-park-republic-k (accessed January 11, 2016).

increase the potential of either sanctions or other means" to alter Kim Jong-un's behavior. In September 2015, Secretary Kerry warned of "severe consequences" if North Korea "refuses to live up to its international obligations."[44]

Myth 5. Sanctions do not work. Tougher measures were effective when applied. In 2005, the U.S. designated Banco Delta Asia (BDA) as a money-laundering concern[45] for facilitating North Korean illicit activities and banned all U.S. financial institutions from dealing with the Macau bank. The U.S. Department of the Treasury also considered implementing similar measures against other, larger banks, including the Macao branch of the Bank of China, against which it had "voluminous" evidence. However, the Bush Administration reportedly refrained to "avoid excessive damage to the financial system of Macao and a resultant clash with China."[46]

North Korea was shunned by the international financial system due to the cumulative effect of the action, the clear signal that Washington would belatedly begin enforcing its laws, and a series of *sub rosa* meetings by U.S. officials throughout Asia. Two dozen financial institutions voluntarily cut back or terminated their business with North Korea, including institutions in China, Japan, Vietnam, Mongolia, and Singapore.[47] BDA targeted financial measures showed the efficacy of economic pressure tactics on North Korea. A North Korean negotiator admitted to a senior White House official, "You finally found a way to hurt us."[48]

At the time, critics derided the BDA law enforcement initiative as a neoconservative attempt to undermine the six-party nuclear negotiations. Yet senior Obama Administration officials privately characterized the initiative as having been "very effective" and argued that President George Bush's decision to rescind it was "a mistake that eased pressure on Pyongyang before it took irreversible steps to dismantle its nuclear program."[49] The Obama Administration now "hopes to recreate the financial pressure that North Korea endured back in 2005 when [the United States] took the action against Banco Delta Asia."[50]

Myth 6. China would never go along with targeted financial measures. China has shown itself to be part of the problem rather than part of the solution by turning a blind eye to North Korean proliferation crossing China and not fully implementing U.N. measures. But as former Treasury Department official Juan Zarate commented in his book *Treasury's War*, the U.S.

[44]"Kerry Warns N.Korea of 'Severe Consequences' over Nukes," *The Chosun Ilbo*, September 18, 2015.
[45]Under the Patriot Act, § 311, 31 U.S. Code § 5318A.
[46]Donald Greenlees and David Lague, "The Money Trail That Linked North Korea to Macao," *The New York Times*, April 11, 2007. http://www.nytimes.com/2007/04/11/world/asia/11cnd-macao.html?_r=0 (accessed January 12, 2016.
[47]Daniel L. Glaser, testimony before the Committee on Banking, Housing, and Urban Affairs, U.S. Senate, September 12, 2006,
http://www.banking.senate.gov/public/index.cfm?FuseAction=Files.View&FileStore_id=deda4b45-d225-4a22-8cc4-2154cbc61dcd (accessed January 11, 2016).
[48]Juan Zarate, *Treasury's War: The Unleashing of a New Era of Financial Warfare* (New York: Public Affairs, 2013).
[49]Jay Solomon, "U.S. Pursues Financial Leverage over North Korea," *The Wall Street Journal*, July 1, 2009, http://online.wsj.com/article/SB124632106686771095.html (accessed January 11, 2016).
[50]Margaret Brenan, "U.S. Urges Nations to Cut North Korea's Financial Link," CBS News, April 5, 2013, http://webcache.googleusercontent.com/search?q=cache:n3xFhCyg6QAJ:www.cbsnews.com/8301-202_162-57578210/u.s-urges-nations-to-cut-north-koreas-financial-link (accessed January 11, 2016).

action on Banco Delta Asia compelled Chinese banks to make a choice—appear legitimate by scrutinizing North Korean illicit financial activity in their banks, or risk becoming a financial rogue and losing access to the U.S. financial system.

As Zarate points out, it became apparent that Chinese financial entities could be persuaded to follow the U.S. Treasury's lead and act against their government's own stated foreign policy and political interests.

Hitting the Snooze Bar on North Korean Sanctions

While implementing new sanctions measures is important, fully implementing and enforcing already existing far-reaching measures is as important, if not more critical. For years, the Obama Administration has vowed that it is contemplating additional sanctions measures but instead pursued a policy of timid incrementalism. Strong vows to act resolutely were not backed up by strong actions.

Unilateral U.S. actions against Iran, combined with diplomatic pressure, led other nations to impose their own financial and regulatory measures against Tehran. Collectively, the international sanctions isolated Iran from the international banking system, targeted critical Iranian economic sectors, and forced countries to restrict purchases of Iranian oil and gas, Tehran's largest export.

Just as strong measures induced Iran back to the negotiating table, more robust measures are needed to leverage North Korea. The United States should use its action against Iran as a model for imposing the same severity of targeted financial measures against North Korea.

However, by instead pulling our legal punches but always promising to be tougher "the next time," Washington squandered the opportunity to more effectively impede progress on North Korea's nuclear and missile programs and coerce compliance with U.N. resolutions. The collective international finger-wagging and promises to be tougher the next time have allowed North Korea additional years to develop and refine its nuclear weapons and the means to deliver them. Pyongyang feels that its own strategic patience policy can outlast that of the United States.

Washington should no longer hold some sanctions in abeyance, to be rolled out after the next North Korean violation or provocation. There will be little change until North Korea feels pain and China feels concern over the consequences of Pyongyang's actions and its own obstructionism. The U.S. needs to sharpen the choices for North Korea by raising the risk and cost for those violating laws and resolutions and who have been willing so far to facilitate North Korea's prohibited programs and illicit activities.

U.S. actions can have ripple effects by altering the cost–benefit analysis of those engaging with North Korean shady entities as well as induce other nations to duplicate American law enforcement actions.

What Should Be Done
The United States should increase punitive measures against North Korea, including enhancing sanctions to the same degree as they have been applied against other rogue regimes.

In the U.N., the U.S. should press the Security Council to:

- **Close loopholes in Resolution 2094,** such as including Article 42 of Chapter VII of the U.N. Charter, which allows for enforcement by military means. This would authorize naval ships to intercept, board, and inspect North Korean ships suspected of transporting precluded nuclear, missile, and conventional arms, components, or technology.
- **Adopt a more comprehensive list of prohibited items and materials.** The U.N. Experts Group identified several items and materials critical to Pyongyang's nuclear programs that should be—but have not been—added to the list of products banned for transfer to North Korea. These include maraging steel, frequency changers (also known as converters or inverters), high-strength aluminum alloy, filament winding machines, ring magnets, and semi-hard magnetic alloys in thin strip form.[51]
- **Consider constraining trade of major North Korean imports and exports.** The U.S. should apply sanctions similar to those imposed on significant Iranian imports and exports. The U.S. should also restrict North Korean energy imports and the export of North Korean resources. U.S. law restricts access to the U.S. financial system by foreign companies and banks if they do business with Iran's energy sector or process petroleum transactions with Iran's central bank.

The United States should unilaterally:

- **Designate North Korea as a primary money-laundering concern.** In 2002, 2004, and 2011, the U.S. Treasury designated Ukraine, Burma, and Iran, respectively, as "jurisdiction[s] of primary money laundering concern."[52]
- **Ban North Korean financial institutions' correspondent accounts[53] in the United States.** Designating North Korea as a money-laundering concern would prohibit North Korea from "the opening or maintaining in the United States of a correspondent account or payable-through account by any domestic financial institution or domestic financial agency for or on behalf of a foreign banking institution."[54]
- **Publicly identify and sanction all foreign companies, financial institutions, and governments assisting North Korea's nuclear and missile programs.** Executive Orders 13382 and 13551 enable targeted financial and regulatory measures, including freezing of assets, against any entity suspected of helping North Korean nuclear, missile, and conventional arms; criminal activities; money laundering; or import of luxury goods.

---

[51]U.N. Panel of Experts, "Report of the Panel of Experts Established Pursuant to Resolution 1874 (2009)," http://www.ncnk.org/resources/publications/UN-Panel-of-Experts-Report-May-2011.pdf/.

[52]U.S. Department of the Treasury, "Imposition of Special Measures Against Burma." April 2, 2004, *Federal Register*, Vol. 69, No. 70 (April 12, 2004), pp. 19093–19098, http://www.fincen.gov/statutes_regs/patriot/pdf/burma.pdf (accessed September 26. 2013). and press release, "Fact Sheet: New Sanctions on Iran," U.S. Department of the Treasury, November 21. 2011, http://www.treasury.gov/press-center/press-releases/Pages/tg1367.aspx (accessed January 11, 2016).

[53]"Foreign financial institutions maintain accounts at U.S. banks to gain access to the U.S. financial system and to take advantage of services and products that may not be available in the foreign financial institution's jurisdiction." Federal Financial Institutions Examination Council, Bank Secrecy Act/Anti-Money Laundering InfoBase, s.v., "Correspondent Accounts (Foreign)—Overview," http://www.ffiec.gov/bsa_aml_infobase/pages_manual/OLM_047.htm (accessed January 11, 2016).

[54]U.S. Department of the Treasury, Financial Crimes Enforcement Network, "Section 311—Special Measures," http://www.fincen.gov/statutes_regs/patriot/section311.html (accessed January 11. 2016).

The U.S. should call on foreign banks, businesses, and governments to reciprocate U.S. actions against North Korean and foreign violators.

- **Impose third-party sanctions.** The U.S. should penalize entities, particularly Chinese financial institutions and businesses, that trade with those on the sanctions list or export prohibited items. The U.S. should also ban financial institutions that conduct business with North Korea from conducting business in the United States.[55]
- **Compel the removal of North Korea from SWIFT financial transfers.** The Obama Administration and European Union pressured the Belgian-based Society for Worldwide Interbank Financial Telecommunication (SWIFT) to disconnect sanctioned Iranian banks in 2012. The system is the world hub for electronic financial transactions.
- **Urge the European Union and other countries to sever ties with North Korea's Foreign Trade Bank.** The Foreign Trade Bank, North Korea's main financial portal for international trade, was blacklisted by the U.S. and China in 2013 for facilitating North Korean nuclear and missile proliferation.
- **Target the North Korean government writ large, not just individuals or departments.** The U.S. determined in Executive Order 13551 that the North Korean government itself was involved in illicit and deceptive activities.[56]
- **Formally charge North Korea as a currency counterfeiter.** U.S. officials have repeatedly declared that North Korea is counterfeiting U.S. currency.[57] Under international law, counterfeiting of a country's currency "qualifies as a proxy attack on its national integrity and sovereignty—and a *causus belli* to justify self-defense."[58]
- **Return North Korea to the state sponsors of terrorism list.** Inclusion on the list requires the U.S. government to oppose loans by international financial institutions, such as the World Bank, International Monetary Fund, and Asian Development Bank.[59]
- **Tighten maritime counterproliferation.** The U.S. should target shipping companies and airlines caught proliferating such as Air Koryo. If they are state-owned, the U.S. should sanction the relevant government ministry. Sanctions have been applied against the Islamic Republic of Iran Shipping Line and Iran Air.
- **Enhance U.S. inspection of shipping companies transiting ports that consistently fail to inspect North Korean cargo.** Any vessel or aircraft that has transported prohibited North Korean items should be seized upon entering U.S. jurisdiction.

---

[55]Executive Order 13551 applies U.S. sanctions to anyone who has assisted "any person whose property and interests in property are blocked pursuant to this order." Barack Obama, "Blocking Property of Certain Persons with Respect to North Korea," Executive Order 13551, § 1(a)(ii) (E). http://www.whitehouse.gov/the-press-office/2010/08/30/executive-order-president-blocking-property-certain-persons-with-respect (accessed January 11, 2016).

[56]Executive Order 13551 concludes by "finding that the continued actions and policies of the Government of North Korea, [including] its illicit and deceptive activities in international markets through which it obtains financial and other support, including money laundering, the counterfeiting of goods and currency, bulk cash smuggling, and narcotics trafficking...constitute an unusual and extraordinary threat to the national security, foreign policy, and economy of the United States." Ibid. (emphasis added).

[57]Phillip Crowley, daily press briefing, U.S. Department of State, August 2, 2010, http://www.state.gov/r/pa/prs/dpb/2010/08/145491.htm (accessed January 11, 2016).

[58]Zarate, *Treasury's War.*

[59]Section 1621, "Opposition to Assistance by International Financial Institutions to Terrorist States," International Financial Institutions Act (Public Law 95–118), as cited in Mark E. Manyin, "North Korea: Back on the Terrorism List?" Congressional Research Service *Report for Congress*, June 29, 2010, http://www.nkeconwatch.com/nk-uploads/DPRK-back-on-terrorism-list.pdf (accessed January 11, 2016).

- **Implement sanctions for human rights violations.** Impose targeted financial measures against all North Korean entities—and their leadership—identified by the commission and then call upon other nations to take commensurate action.
- **Publicly highlight Chinese obstructionism** to addressing North Korea's heinous human rights abuses and Beijing's complicity through forced repatriation of refugees in violation of several international accords.
- **Fully fund U.S. defense requirements.** It is unrealistic to think that the United States can cut defense spending by $1 trillion over the next decade and still maintain its current level of commitment and deterrence.

For its part, South Korea should:
- **Expand the scope of recently resumed propaganda broadcasts** along the demilitarized zone. These efforts should include assessing the viability of expanding cell phone signals into North Korea, using drones along North Korean coasts, and removing any restrictions on nongovernment organizations sending information leaflets via balloons into North Korea. The August land mine crisis showed the sensitivity of the Kim Jong-un regime to psychological operations.
- **Sever its involvement in the Kaesong industrial park.** The joint business venture was always more focused on political than economic objectives. Since its inception, the Kaesong venture failed to achieve its primary objective of inducing economic and political reform in North Korea and moderating the regime's belligerent foreign policy.
- **Request U.S. deployment of the terminal high altitude air defense (THAAD) missile defense system.** South Korea's indigenous missile defense system is insufficient to defend against North Korea's growing nuclear and missile threat.
- **Pass its first North Korean Human Rights Act,** which would provide funding for human rights groups and impose conditions on engagement with Pyongyang. The National Assembly has debated legislation for ten years—it is time to act.

Conclusion

North Korea's nuclear test is a flagrant violation of numerous U.N. Security Council resolutions. It reflects Pyongyang's continued pursuit of its prohibited nuclear weapons programs in open defiance of the international community despite countless attempts by the U.S. and its allies to reach a diplomatic resolution.

The regime has repeatedly asserted it has no intention of ever abandoning its nuclear weapons, even revising its constitution to enshrine itself as a nuclear weapons state. North Korea's continuing improvement and augmentation of its nuclear arsenal threatens the U.S. and its allies. It is time for the Obama Administration to abandon its policy of timid incrementalism and fully implement existing U.S. laws by imposing stronger sanctions on North Korea and to work with Congress to determine additional measures.

Neither sanctions nor diplomacy alone is a panacea, both are essential and mutually supporting elements of a comprehensive integrated strategy utilizing all the instruments of national power. The U.S. has strong tools, it has just lacked the resolve to use them.

The imperative question would be, "Why has the United States hesitated to impose the same legal measures against North Korea that it has already used against other countries for far less egregious violations of U.S. and international law?"

Mr. SALMON. Thank you.
Ms. Glaser.

STATEMENT OF MS. BONNIE GLASER, SENIOR ADVISER FOR ASIA, DIRECTOR OF CHINA POWER PROJECT, CENTER FOR STRATEGIC AND INTERNATIONAL STUDIES

Ms. GLASER. Chairman Salmon, Ranking Member Sherman, and distinguished members of the subcommittee, I am honored to have the opportunity to testify today on this very important issue.

As so many of you have already pointed out, cooperation from China, North Korea's main benefactor, is essential to achieving a nuclear-free peninsula. China is North Korea's biggest trading partner. It accounts for 90 percent of North Korea's global trade, provides at least 70 percent of North Korea's crude oil requirements, some 80 percent of its consumer goods, approximately 45 percent of its food, and Chinese investment accounts for almost 95 percent of foreign direct investment in North Korea.

The U.S. should not expect Beijing to completely abandon its ally and forge a common strategy with Washington to squeeze North Korea until it gives up its nuclear weapons or collapses. But it may be possible to persuade China to strictly comply with its existing international commitments to further tighten sanctions on North Korea and to reduce its support or make continued support contingent on specific actions by Pyongyang to return to its denuclearization pledges.

To elicit greater cooperation, the U.S. must attach high priority to North Korea on the U.S.-China agenda, especially in summit meetings between our Presidents, U.S. and Chinese leaders. Cooperation on North Korea should be identified as a litmus test of the proposition that the United States and China can work together where their interests overlap, and the U.S. should then take the following steps.

First, the U.S. should call out China for its failure to enforce existing U.N. sanctions. North Korea has deep networks with Chinese companies and uses these relationships to procure prohibited items from all over the world, routing them through China before onward shipment to North Korea. Designated North Korean entities continue to do business with Chinese companies and visit Chinese ports. North Koreans are reportedly still able to conduct banking transactions in small banks operating in Northeast China along the border. China does not enforce the ban on luxury goods.

Second, the U.S. should press Beijing to agree to the designation of more North Korean individuals and entities in new U.N. Security Council resolution.

Third, the U.S. should encourage Beijing to use its leverage over North Korea in targeted ways to pressure for change in its behavior. China could refuse to engage in new economic projects with North Korea until the government returns to negotiations in good faith. Beijing could reduce the flow of Chinese tourists to North Korea, which has become a significant source of foreign exchange.

Fourth, the United States should encourage China to leverage its assistance to North Korea to influence its behavior. So to deter North Korean long-range missile launches and nuclear tests, China could agree to warn Pyongyang that future provocations would be followed by a cutback in Chinese aid. Beijing could also insist that Pyongyang return to its commitments under the Six Party talks or face substantial reductions in deliveries of crude oil, kerosene, diesel, and gasoline.

And, fifth, the U.S. should press China to not obstruct discussion in U.N. bodies on human rights abuses in North Korea. And my colleague, Victor Cha, has already underscored North Korea's sensitivity to this issue.

Securing cooperation from China to increase pressure on North Korea may be more feasible than in the past. Xi Jinping is a decisive and bold leader who has a clear vision of what is needed to achieve what he calls the ''Chinese dream,'' the great rejuvenation of the Chinese nation. And under Xi's leadership, China has embarked on an effort to end the special relationship of the past between Beijing and Pyongyang and replace it with a normal state-to- state relationship.

Widely viewed as the most powerful leader China has had since Deng Xiaoping, Xi Jinping has sufficient clout to overrule opposition from potent constituencies in China that would resist a tougher stance toward North Korea, especially in the party and the military.

Beijing is not prepared to assume sole responsibility for addressing the North Korean nuclear threat, but China might be willing to do more along the lines that I have outlined if it believes that the U.S. has an effective strategy, is prioritizing the goal of creating a non-nuclear Korean peninsula, and does not seek to use the Korean peninsula to harm Chinese interests.

What does China want? A balance of power in Northeast Asia that is favorable to Chinese interests, and certainly does not threaten Chinese interests.

I believe China does not adamantly oppose Korean unification, but the known burdens and dangers of the status quo today are less risky for China than the uncertainty that unification may bring for Chinese interests.

And I look forward to the discussion. Thank you again.

[The prepared statement of Ms. Glaser follows:]

Statement before the
House Committee on Foreign Affairs,
Subcommittee on Asia and the Pacific

"THE US RESPONSE TO NORTH KOREA'S NUCLEAR PROVOCATIONS"

A Testimony by:

Bonnie S. Glaser

Senior Adviser for Asia and

Director, China Power Project

Center for Strategic and International Studies (CSIS)

January 13, 2016

Chairman Salmon, Ranking Member Sherman and Distinguished Members of the Subcommittee:

I am honored to have this opportunity to discuss the US response to North Korea's nuclear provocations. I commend the Subcommittee for convening this timely hearing to assess whether US strategy toward North Korea is on the right track and what steps might be taken to advance the goal of eliminating North Korea's nuclear programs. My testimony today will focus primarily on the role of China in the overall effort to mount an effective strategy to dismantle North Korea's nuclear capabilities.

North Korea's fourth nuclear test conducted on January 5 is just the latest reminder of the danger posed to the international community by Pyongyang's nuclear programs. Regardless of how successful the test is judged to have been, it underscores that the policies pursued by the United States and other countries have failed to make progress toward the complete, verifiable and irreversible denuclearization of the Korean Peninsula. The US and its allies and partners have been unable to persuade North Korea that abandoning its nuclear weapons would enhance its security. On the contrary, Pyongyang has continued to take steps to further develop its nuclear and ballistic missile capabilities in defiance of numerous UN Security Council Resolutions.

A crucial element of US strategy to convince North Korea to give up its nuclear weapons is working with key members of the international community to tighten national and international sanctions. Cooperation from China, North Korea's main and almost sole remaining benefactor, is essential to achieving this goal. China is North Korea's biggest trading partner, accounting for 90 percent of North Korea's global trade. Official two-way trade between China and North Korea continues to grow, reaching $6.97 billion in 2014. China is a treaty ally of Pyongyang and remains committed to rendering military and other assistance to North Korea in the event of armed attack. Beijing is the also most important source of North Korea's food, and energy, including kerosene for aircraft fuel. China provides over 70 percent of North Korea's crude oil requirements, some 80 percent of its consumer goods, and approximately 45 percent of its food. Chinese investment accounts for almost 95 percent of foreign direct investment in North Korea.

At the United Nations, China has agreed to increasingly punitive measures by the international community on Pyongyang since 2006, when North Korea undertook missile tests and first tested a nuclear weapon. Following North Korea's second nuclear test in May 2009 and its third test in February 2013, Beijing voted in favor of tightening sanctions. It also supported sanctions after an attempted satellite launch in December 2012. Yet China's support of all the above resolutions came at the price of a reduction in the scope of the sanctions. China's willingness to support UN sanctions has been strictly limited to the transfer or sale of military and WMD-related items. It has vigorously opposed imposing economic sanctions on North Korea, agreeing only to target luxury goods.

Moreover, China's enforcement of UN sanctions remains inadequate. North Korea has deep networks with Chinese companies and uses these relationships to procure prohibited items from all over the world, routing them through China before onward shipment to North Korea. Designated North Korea entities continue to do business with Chinese companies and visit Chinese ports. North Koreans are reportedly still able to conduct banking transactions in small banks operating in northeast China along the border. China does not enforce the mandated ban on luxury goods. Chinese customs data shows that North Korea imported $2.09 billion worth of luxury goods between 2012 and 2014.

In addition to blocking any economic sanctions from UN resolutions, China has also occasionally shielded North Korea from international criticism of its violations of human rights and its flagrant provocations against South Korea. In March 2010, Beijing refused to condemn Pyongyang despite conclusive evidence that demonstrated the North's responsibility for the sinking of a South Korean naval vessel. In February 2014, China criticized a UN report that detailed human rights atrocities in North Korea. In December 2015, China, along with Russia, attempted to block UN Security Council discussions on North Korea's human rights abuses.

There have been some indications, however, that Chinese President Xi Jinping is more willing than his predecessors to put pressure on North Korea. In recent years China has apparently stepped up interceptions of weapons-related materials being transshipped through China into North Korea. China has also undertaken periodic unilateral measures to signal its displeasure to Pyongyang. Soon after the February

2013 nuclear test, small steps were taken to restrict inter-banking arrangements with North Korea's main foreign exchange bank. In another sign of China's growing concern about North Korea's nuclear ambitions, the Chinese government published a long list of equipment and chemical substances banned from export to North Korea in September 2013.

There are several reasons for Beijing's unwillingness to support crippling economic sanctions against North Korea and for its continuing overall support for the Kim dynasty. From China's perspective, sanctions and other forms of pressure must be part of a broader strategy that includes positive inducements and dialogue. Such a "grand bargain" might include security assurances, economic assistance, and diplomatic recognition by the United States and Japan. Sanctions alone, the Chinese believe, are unlikely to persuade Pyongyang to denuclearize. Moreover, although China opposes Pyongyang's nuclear weapons program, its willingness to pressure North Korea to denuclearize is limited to measures that will not undermine stability in North Korea. Despite ample evidence that Chinese President Xi Jinping has great contempt for Kim Jung-un and his policies, Beijing remains wary of the risks to Chinese security of regime collapse in North Korea. One such threat is a chaotic influx of North Korean refugees into China. Even more worrisome to Beijing is the possibility that rapid Korean unification could result in the deployment of American troops north of the 38th parallel and an even more unfavorable balance of power in Northeast Asia. Beijing prefers that Korean unification be postponed until China can neutralize the US-ROK alliance. The bottom line is that at least for the time being, Beijing judges that the uncertain risks of unification are greater than the known burdens and dangers of the status quo.

In the face of only limited, episodic pressure from the international community, China will continue on its current course of calling for a nuclear-free Korean Peninsula, occasionally prodding Pyongyang to implement economic reform while working to prevent a regime collapse. On the diplomatic front, the Chinese will continue to attempt to create conditions for reconvening the Six Party Talks, which they insist is the only mechanism that can produce a peaceful, negotiated settlement to the North Korea nuclear issue. As long as rolling back Pyongyang's nuclear weapons program remains a relatively low priority in Washington, it is certain that China will not be compelled to change its calculus or its policy. Many Chinese experts have concluded that the US is willing to live with a nuclear-armed

Korea as long as Pyongyang does not proliferate nuclear material outside its borders.

What Can the US Persuade China to Do and How?

The US-China relationship is increasingly competitive and in some areas is potentially antagonistic. Competition is especially intense in the Asia-Pacific region, where China seeks to weaken US alliances, undermine American credibility, and create an integrated, interconnected region with China at its center. Nevertheless, the U.S.-China relationship is not a zero-sum game. Cooperation between Beijing and Washington is possible where US and Chinese interests converge or overlap sufficiently to enable agreement on joint or parallel steps toward a common objective. In the case of North Korea, the US should not expect China to abandon its ally and forge a common strategy with Washington to squeeze North Korea until it gives up its nuclear weapons or collapses. But it may be possible to persuade Beijing to strictly comply with its existing international commitments, to further tighten sanctions on North Korea, and to reduce its support or make continued support contingent on specific actions by Pyongyang to return to its denuclearization pledges.

The first step that must be taken by the US to elicit greater Chinese cooperation is to attach high priority to North Korea on the bilateral agenda and especially in summit meetings between US and Chinese leaders. Washington must alter Beijing's perception that US strategy toward North Korea, which has been dubbed by many as "strategic patience," means that the Obama administration has put North Korea on the back burner and is willing to tolerate North Korea's defiance of international sanctions. Once the message is conveyed that cooperation on North Korea is a litmus test of the proposition that the US and China can work together where they share common interests, Washington should seek to achieve the following specific goals with China:

Compliance with Existing International Commitments

The US should publicly identify and consider sanctioning China for its failure to enforce UN sanctions. Under existing executive orders, the US president can take action against any entity suspected of helping North Korean nuclear, missile, and conventional military programs; criminal activities; money laundering or import of luxury goods. The president can also penalize Chinese financial institutions and businesses that trade with North Korean entities on the sanctions list or export prohibited items.

There are numerous examples of Chinese non-compliance with UN sanctions on North Korea. For example, according to the 2015 report by the UNSCR 1874 Panel of Experts, Chinese companies have provided the autopilot component for drones sold to North Korea that have conducted reconnaissance activities over military facilities on Republic of Korea territory. The same report cites China as the source of ski lift equipment to a ski resort in North Korea. Apparently China claims that such equipment does not fall under the prohibited luxury goods specified in Security Council resolution 2094. In addition, the UN Panel of Experts report provides evidence that Chinese companies continue to do business with Ocean Maritime Management Company, Limited (OMM), which has been subject to UN sanctions since July 2014. Washington could publicly condemn China for permitting North Korea to use its airspace, land border, and waters to transfer illicit items to other countries in violation of UN Security Council resolutions.

In a few months, the UNSC Panel of Experts will release its 2016 report. It is expected to contain more instances of Chinese violations of UN sanctions. The US has been reluctant to publicly criticize China for these breaches because it needs to keep Beijing on board in order to isolate North Korea with unanimous Security Council resolutions and also to avoid undermining cooperation with China in other arenas. If it is now time to end "business as usual" with North Korea, as Secretary of State John Kerry has stated, then it is necessary for China to comply with all existing UN sanctions.

Expand Sanctions on North Korea

The US should press Beijing to agree to the designation of more North Korean individuals and entities in a new UN Security Council resolution. After Pyongyang's April 2012 missile launch, the US, South Korea, Japan and the EU proposed adding 40 additional North Korean entities to the UN sanctions list, but China vetoed all but three. In 2013, US and South Korean authorities uncovered dozens of overseas bank accounts worth hundreds of millions of dollars that were linked to top North Korean leaders, which they proposed including in UN sanctions lists, but Beijing refused. China has also strongly opposed levying sanctions on high-level North Korean officials such as the head of the North Korea's agency responsible for conducting its nuclear tests.

Implementation of Unilateral Steps to Curb Economic Interaction with North Korea

The US should encourage Beijing to use its leverage over North Korea in targeted ways to pressure for changes in its behavior. China could refuse to engage in new economic projects with North Korea until the government returns to negotiations in good faith. The Chinese government could direct Chinese companies to curtail business with North Korea. There are allegedly more than 200 Chinese companies that operate in North Korea in mining, industrial parts and materials, agriculture and timber, transportation, apparel, consumer goods, iron and steel, and automotive vehicles and parts. Chinese companies could forego new investments for an indefinite period, not simply postpone new projects for a limited period of time as occurred after Pyongyang's third nuclear test in February 2013.

China could also halt the flow of Chinese tourists to North Korea, which has become a significant source of foreign exchange. In 2014 North Korea's estimated income from foreign tourists was between $30.6 and $43.6 million, with 95,000 of the approximately 100,000 tourists coming from China. In a drive backed by Kim Jong-un to expand the tourism sector, North Korea hopes to attract a million visitors by 2017 and two million by 2020.

Chinese banks could be vigorously discouraged from doing business with North Korea. As demonstrated when the US Department of the Treasury designated Banco Delta Asia as a "primary money laundering concern" under Section 311 of the USA PATRIOT Act in 2005, China can be incentivized to curb its financial transactions with North Korea when forced to choose between business as usual with North Korea and losing access to the US banking and financial system. The Chinese government should also be pressed to shut down the grey market in which Chinese private firms engage in transactions with North Korean state trade companies within China's national economy. Financial transactions are increasingly being undertaken outside major Chinese banks through third countries,

Chinese local banks, or by avoiding the banking system altogether. China's local and central governments have turned a blind eye to these developments.

Tie Aid to Denuclearization Steps

The US should encourage China to leverage its assistance to North Korea to influence its behavior. To deter North Korean long-range missile launches and nuclear tests, China could agree to warn Pyongyang that future provocations would be followed by a cut back in Chinese aid. Beijing could also insist that Pyongyang return to its commitments under the September 2005 Six Party Talks agreement or face substantial reductions in deliveries of crude oil, kerosene, diesel, and gasoline. North Korea's economy would grind to a halt without energy assistance from China. Beijing has previously halted supplies of oil for limited periods. In March 2003, for example, China shut down the oil pipeline from Liaoning province to North Korea for three days shortly after Pyongyang test-fired missiles into waters between the Korean Peninsula and Japan. China has also significantly reduced exports to North Korea of kerosene for jet fuel in recent years, though whether this is part of strategy to pressure North Korea is unknown. According to customs statistics, China halted crude oil shipments to North Korea in December 2013, but there is evidence that a DPRK crude oil tanker has loaded oil in Dalian and made deliveries to North Korean refineries. Some observers also suspect that China is providing crude oil in the form of economic aid rather than as exports.

Stop Blocking International Pressure on North Korea on Human Rights

The US should press China to not obstruct discussion in United Nations bodies on human rights abuses in North Korea. It is apparent that the Kim Jung-un regime is sensitive to human rights, especially the possibility that its leader may face official international condemnation. This is a potential source of leverage that the Obama administration should seek to use to influence North Korea. China should also be called on to end its practice of sending North Korean refugees back to their country, where they can face imprisonment and torture.

Cooperation to Reduce North Korea's Illicit Activity

The US should put pressure on China to work with the US, Japan, South Korea, and other countries to require inspections of all vessels and aircraft arriving from

North Korea. Stepped up inspections could significantly reduce Pyongyang's illicit shipments of drugs and counterfeit money, as well as the North's ability to procure materials for its missile and nuclear weapons programs. The US should also renew efforts to urge China to join the Proliferation Security Initiative (PSI) which was created in 2003 to interdict shipments of WMD and related materials to terrorists and countries of proliferation concern. Beijing's main objection to PSI is that its members might be subject to interdiction in situations that China considers to be "innocent passage," which it argues constitutes a violation of international law. Although China has refused to join PSI, the Chinese government has stated clearly that it shares the non-proliferation goal PSI.

Improved Prospects for Gaining Chinese Cooperation

Securing cooperation from China to increase pressure on North Korea may be more feasible than in the past. While Beijing will likely continue to oppose crippling economic sanctions that pose a risk of bringing down Kim Jong-un's regime, there are moderately good prospects for gaining Chinese support for a range of steps to intensify pressure on Pyongyang on the nuclear front. As a result of the rapid improvement in Chinese ties with South Korea and the growth in Chinese confidence in its own rising power, Beijing may be less committed than in the past to preserving a buffer between Chinese territory and democratic, pro-American South Korea at all costs. The strategic liability of North Korea as an ally is likely becoming abundantly clear to Beijing. North Korea's nuclear weapons development and other provocations have provided the US and its allies the rationale to increase missile defense deployments, stage more frequent and more robust military exercises, strengthen regional alliances, enhance trilateral cooperation among the US, Japan and the ROK, and deepen the US rebalance to Asia. China's leaders are likely painfully aware that if the North retains and continues to expand its nuclear weapons arsenal, Japan, South Korea and possibly other countries in the region might seek their own nuclear weapons capability.

Xi Jinping is a decisive and bold leader who has a clear vision of what is needed to achieve what he calls the Chinese Dream—the great rejuvenation of the Chinese nation. Under Xi's leadership, China has embarked on an effort to end the "special relationship" of the past between Beijing and Pyongyang and replace it with a "normal" state-to-state relationship that better serves Chinese interests. Xi has unabashedly demonstrated a preference for closer relations with Seoul over Pyongyang, meeting six times with ROK President Park Geun-hye while snubbing Kim Jong-un. Xi has little patience for Kim, who is less predictable than his father and more willing to defy North Korea's primary patron. Widely viewed as the most power leader China has had since Deng Xiaoping, Xi likely has sufficient clout to overrule opposition from potent constituencies in China that would resist a tougher stance toward North Korea, especially in the party and the military.

A major obstacle to greater US-Chinese cooperation on North Korea is China's skepticism that the US has an effective strategy and the political will to implement it. To gain greater cooperation from China, the US will need to put forward a concrete plan that contains incentives to Pyongyang to dismantle its nuclear programs in addition to coercive measures to apply if its refuses. Beijing is not prepared to assume sole responsibility for addressing the North Korea nuclear problem, but it might work with a US administration that is determined to resolve the North Korea nuclear threat once and for all.

Mr. SALMON. Thank you. I would like to thank the distinguished panel members very much for making the time to be here today. You know, it is kind of unnerving when Seth Rogen gets more reaction out of the North Koreans than our American policies do. He certainly hit a nerve, you know, when he put that movie out, a lot more than any of the blustering that has been coming out of Washington, DC.

It has been a conundrum, as pointed out by my colleague, Dana Rohrabacher, that is not new. It is not an issue that was resolved at one time and has degraded. It has never been resolved. And every time I have spoken with any expert about how to get North Korea to start living with accepted international norms, especially when it comes to proliferation, every one of those conversations always involves China, because they are the 800-pound gorilla when it comes to dealing with North Korea, because of North Korea's dependence on them for food and energy.

And, Ms. Glaser, you have made some very I think astute observations on what China could do. But how do we motivate them properly to get that done? There have been a lot of things talked about—maybe targeted sanctions that involve Chinese banks that fund North Korea. Maybe that is something we can look at. I spoke to Mr. Sherman about that, maybe looking at that in a bipartisan way.

Mr. Klingner, you have said that in your submitted speech, your written speech, you are going to be talking about several of the sanctions that maybe could and should be on the table. I would like us to really look at entertaining those. I think that the bill that was passed yesterday on the House floor was a good move. I think it moves the ball up the field. But I think there is even more to be done.

You have pointed out, rightly so, Mr. Klingner, that we haven't even considered or done similar things that we have done to far less egregious offenders in the world today. And I think that is abominable. I think we should put all things on the table.

I would like to ask you, Mr. Klingner, why do you think that there has been such restraint on dealing with North Korea in the same way that we have dealt with far less offenders? What is the rationale? It doesn't make any sense to me. Why have we been so reticent to do so?

Mr. KLINGNER. That is an excellent question, sir, which I really don't have an answer to. It really is counterintuitive. You know, if you just compare Iran and North Korea, Iran remains in the Non-Proliferation Treaty. North Korea is out. Iran claims that its nuclear program is for civilian purposes. North Korea quite clearly says it is to incinerate the U.S. and its allies. Iran, you know, has not exploded a nuclear device. North Korean has done four.

And Iran has oil. One would think that we would have more pressure on North Korea than Iran, but we haven't. There are perhaps the concerns as to how North Korea will respond if we impose additional measures. I don't think we should be hesitant to enforce our laws because of the concerns of what the criminal will do if we enforce them.

Similarly, as has already been talked about, is how will China respond? When I advocated additional measures against North

Korea, I have said, "Let the law enforcement people go where the evidence takes them." And someone once commented to me that, "Oh, so you want to sacrifice the all-important U.S.-China relationship over North Korea?"

I said, "Well, no. What I am saying is I don't want to give China immunity from U.S. law simply because they are China." So we should go where the evidence takes us. We should sanction whatever entities are violating U.S. and international law and U.N. resolutions, not because they are Chinese but because they are violating our laws and the resolutions.

Mr. SALMON. I think that your answer kind of dovetails with the opening statement of the ranking member, and I think that these comments really have a lot of bearing on going forward. I think that there really shouldn't be any sacred cows when it comes to enforcing our laws. And protection of special interests or, you know, ongoing concerns over a bilateral relationship with China, these are serious issues. And China has not stood up for its obligations, I believe, in this realm.

One thing that has been mentioned that might get China's attention, and I think it is also just good policy, is what about the U.S. bolstering our support for a missile defense system for South Korea at the least, and maybe Japan? What do you think about that, Dr. Cha and Mr. Klingner?

Mr. CHA. So I think that is a great idea. On the China piece of it, first, as Bruce said, when there was a Section 311 against a Chinese bank in Macao in 2005, that was a law enforcement action. It was a Chinese bank. And, in the end, the U.S.-China relationship survived. So, and it was an effective—it was a very effective measure. And it actually may take things like that to actually motivate China. We are almost self-deterring in that sense, supposed equities in the relationship.

With regard to measures with other countries in the region, I think absolutely this—all of North Korea's activities speak to the need for a much more robust and networked missile defense system in Asia, including the United States, Japan, and South Korea. As was mentioned, the relationship between Japan and Korea has gone through some rough periods, but it is on the mend, and there are I think opportunities here, particularly in South Korea, to talk about more missile defense as well as better intelligence and information-sharing among the three countries.

These have been on our agenda with our allies for quite some time, and we haven't been able to push them forward. And unfortunate as it is, you know, when we were working on the policy every time North Korea did something bad, the motto in the office was, "Well, let's make lemonade out of this lemon." And one of the ways to make lemonade out of this lemon is to really consolidate our defense alliances, and that also complicates the environment for China and may motivate them to do more.

Mr. SALMON. Mr. Klingner.

Mr. KLINGNER. Yes. Last year I wrote a detailed research paper that South Korea should allow the U.S. to deploy THAAD, the Terminal High Altitude Air Defense System. To date, the South Korean administration has not even wanted to publicly discuss it. And, as I pointed out in the paper, THAAD is better than anything the South Koreans have or will have for decades to come. It is more much capable.

Also, I point out that the Chinese claims that it will impair their ability to assault the United States or our allies with missiles, they are red herrings. The THAAD is very effective against North Korean missiles, but it will have no constrainment on Chinese missiles. Therefore, China's objections are politically based.

So I think the U.S., in consultation with our allies, should deploy THAAD. It will improve the defense of not only our forces there, but of South Korea, and also, as Dr. Cha said, to have South Korea integrate its system into the more comprehensive, effective allied system with Japan, because we are all in this together. You know, the same North Korean missile could be aimed on the same trajectory toward South Korea, U.S. Forces in Korea, or U.S. Forces in Japan, which are critical for the defense of the Republic of Korea.

Mr. SALMON. It is no secret that the relationship between China and South Korea has blossomed over the last several years, and they have tried to do everything they can to improve trade, and all aspects of that bilateral relationship. It is also no secret that China has lobbied, and I think that is the understatement of the universe, South Korea against THAAD.

And I think it is time for us, as leaders in the region, to step up our voices and our commitment to security in the region by support for things like that and try to reignite some support for those things, because maybe, just maybe, besides being good policy, from our strategic interests, self-strategic interests, it might be a really good motivation factor for China to finally get off its duff and do something about this serious global problem.

The Chair recognizes Mr. Sherman.

Mr. SHERMAN. Usually it is the witnesses that answer questions. But one question has come up, and that is, why did we do it in Iran and not North Korea? So I think I will answer the question. When Congress passed the sanctions laws, they provided secondary sanctions, which is the only way you go after these regimes. If the law had been enforced it would have made Iran's trading partners very angry.

Administrations refused to enforce those laws, gave Iran a lot more time to get very close to a nuclear weapon, but they began to persuade Iran's trading partners that they should go along with this pressure. And only to the extent that we could carry out the sanctions regime without angering Iran's major trading partners did we carry it out.

And we used persuasion. And who were we persuading? Europe. So we had sanctions on Iran only to the extent that we could get Europe not to be terribly angry if we forced them to go along.

As to China, persuading them will be considerably more difficult. And so the chairman and I are talking about, for example, sanctions on Chinese banks. That will make China angry. In dealing with Iran, the administration got as far as it did without making anybody really angry, any of Iran's trading partners. I think this North Korean nuclear program is significant enough that we should be willing to make China angry.

Now, I might talk about a tariff on their goods that would make them angrier than I could persuade my colleagues in Congress to go along with. But they will be pretty angry with the banking sanctions.

Dr. Cha, you say there are some who doubt that North Korea is legally a terrorist state. One act of terrorism is when you see civilian hostages, and that act of terrorism continues at least until you release the hostages. And if you seize Japanese homemakers and hold them hostage for decades because you want somebody to teach you how to pour tea, that is an act of terrorism.

Dr. Cha, is there any doubt that North Korea is engaged in terrorism until they release the hostages they have seized? Or their bodies, for those who have died?

Mr. CHA. You have no disagreement from me there.

Mr. SHERMAN. Okay.

Mr. CHA. Congressman, I think that there have been many actions in that vein, almost a regular state practice of detaining innocent individuals, Americans and other nationalities, in the country for no apparent reason, and that is just unacceptable.

My only point was that I think that the other area that we could investigate in terms of criteria for putting them back on the list is the cyber area. The——

Mr. SALMON. The cyber terrorism is bad enough. But when you seize people and hold them for decades because you want somebody to teach you a tea ceremony, I have one comment and that is North Korea is very status conscious.

And, of course, the biggest boost to your ego is to have a nuclear-tipped ICBM. The cheesy way to deliver a nuclear weapon is to smuggle one. But I will point out that you can smuggle a nuclear weapon inside a bale of marijuana, and a missile defense program isn't going to stop that.

And, in fact, you have the additional advantage of having plausible deniability or a delay. So retaliation doesn't occur in cold blood. It doesn't occur after a 90-day investigatory process.

I want to go to one more line of questioning. Al-Kibar in Syria, North Korean technology. Just a quick question, does any of our witnesses have any guess as to how much money North Korea was given for cooperating with al-Kibar? I am not seeing any witnesses. But we do—the estimates have been in the hundreds of millions of dollars.

We know two things. Iran wants a nuclear weapon. Iran is about to get its hands on $130 billion. Would North Korea be willing to sell not—they have already proven they are willing to sell nuclear weapons kits, if you will, or equipment and plans. Does North Korea have enough atomic weapons that they would be willing to sell one or two of them? And is this a multi-billion dollar cost for whoever wants to buy them? Do we have—Mr. Klingner.

Mr. KLINGNER. I was going to address your comment about North Korea as a terrorist nation, if I could. In my written testimony, I have a long list of actions that North Korea has taken which I think fulfill the legal obligation for relisting them as a terrorist nation. There are a number of U.S. statutes. Perhaps the most relevant is 18 U.S. Code 2331, which defines international terrorism as "involving violent acts that would be a violation of criminal laws of the U.S., and that appear to be intended to intimidate or coerce a civilian population."

I think the threats of a "9/11-type attack" for citizens of the U.S., or inhabitants of the U.S. to go to theaters to watch that movie, you know, is considered trying to coerce the population. And there have been a number of items that I have listed of North Korean attempts at assassination and kidnapping and that have been recognized by South Korean courts. So I think any one of those should have put North Korea back on the U.S. list, and certainly cumulatively.

As for whether North Korea would sell a nuclear weapon, as you correctly point out, they have shared and sold nuclear and missile technology with a list of rogue nations. I question whether they would sell a completed weapon, though. I think it might go beyond what they would be willing to do, but I certainly could be very wrong on that. Certainly, as they develop a larger arsenal, they might be more willing to do something.

Mr. SHERMAN. What I have said in this room is they need their first 12 atomic weapons to defend themselves from us. The 13th doesn't go on eBay, but could be available for sale.

Dr. Cha.

Mr. CHA. Well, there is certainly a history there. I mean, every major weapon system the North Koreans have ever developed they have sold. And I am——

Mr. SHERMAN. And they haven't drawn the line at nuclear. I mean, had things gone as planned, Syria or Iran operating in combination at al-Kibar would have a plutonium nuclear device. And it is not that North Korea says, "Oh, that is so immoral; we couldn't participate in that."

Mr. CHA. So it is definitely a concern in the case of—as you know well, their missile sales, that has certainly been the case. And, you know, I think part of their effort at trying to develop longer range and more accurate missiles aren't to sell them. So you can't put it past them in terms of the nuclear site.

But even aside from the sort of overt proliferation, just by virtue of the fact that they have a nuclear arsenal that is growing, creates all sort of very serious crisis and stability problems for the United States. I mean, the notion that they can keep a dozen or two dozen bombs, and as long as we deter them we are safe, is completely wrong, because should any crisis develop on the peninsula, North Korea is developing these nuclear capabilities at the expense of massive degrading of their conventional capabilities.

And so what that means is if we are ever in a military crisis, we immediately have to shoot up the escalation ladder, and that immediately forces us to consider preemption. So it is a highly unstable situation that I think gets lost among the general public, because as the chairman said——

Mr. SHERMAN. Doctor, I have gone way over time. I yield back.

Mr. SALMON. I did, too, so I was looking the other way.

The Chair recognizes Mr. Rohrabacher.

Mr. ROHRABACHER. I will try not to go over time. First of all, let me thank the witnesses. Your testimony has been of great value to me and to this committee, and the points that you have made, all of you, I mean, you have made some very serious points and given us information that we will utilize in this coming year as we try to come up with a policy that can deal with this threat.

It is ironic that we seem—I believe the United States and the world is entering a new era. The Cold War is being left behind, a long way, and even the post-Cold War era is being left behind now. And what the new era will be, what is the parameters of how we operate in the world, is going to be different.

And, ironically, the country that may be and the government that may be forcing us into a new definition of what our responsibilities are and what we are going to do is one of the most anachronistic regimes in the world. I mean, they don't even fit into the Cold War, I mean, the way they handle themselves.

I really appreciate the information also about the specifics that the North Korean Government is doing, and the actual people who are running the North Korean Government put up with in terms of the idea of slavery, that they are actually engaged in slavery, which I think there is an important—you have made an important point today. I mean, this is what—that type of activity is intolerable, and those thousands of North Korean workers that are being sent overseas, and all of their salary being given to the government, that is, I believe, virtual slavery.

And thank you for drawing our attention to that. That is something we should be able to deal with, and something we should be able to work with and with international organizations. Let me note that I agree with—and am very pleased that the ranking member, Mr. Sherman, has pointed out that the North Koreans are still holding Japanese hostages after decades. And I agree with him, that should not just be overlooked as if that is a past issue.

The fact that the North Koreans are holding—kidnapped and are holding Japanese civilians in North Korea is something that should be a matter that is not relegated to the past, as long as they are holding these people. And that should be part of what we are looking at.

Whatever we know, whatever era we are entering, we know it is going to be different. And I think that what may come of all of this is that we may find that reunification of Korea becomes a reality after all of these decades, and that reunification will itself create a new world that we have to deal with. We are talking about historic moments in the world. That is where we are at, and it is being brought about by this crazy regime up in North Korea, is forcing these changes upon us.

I would also like to mention that we are now entering an era also where our technology is not just being utilized for offensive weapon systems. And thanks to Ronald Reagan, we started down a path of building and focusing on defensive systems, which make a lot more sense to me, even especially in cases like this where—and let me note there are several new technologies being developed that will give us even a greater ability to defend ourselves against a missile attack. And we certainly should make that available to South Korea and to Japan, and that would certainly be a message there.

Let me ask again for some more information from you folks. Somewhere in the back of my mind is an action that we took, and I believe—and I don't know if it was a covert action, maybe I am just disclosing something—to prevent a transfer of money that was going to specific individuals in the North Korean Government.

We know that North Korea, with all of its poverty and the lack of food, hasn't prevented luxury cars and booze and very expensive consumer items to going to their very elite. And I seem to remember that there were banking transactions that we challenged in some way that had an impact on North Korean policy.

Could you refresh my memory on that? And is that a methodology that we should try to look at now to reestablish that policy toward the new challenge that we face? Dr. Cha.

Mr. CHA. Yes. I think what you are referring to, Congressman, is the Section 311 by the Treasury Department in 2005 that advised U.S. financial institutions not to deal with a particular bank in Macao——

Mr. ROHRABACHER. Macao.

Mr. CHA [continuing]. Because of money laundering concerns. And in the press it is always talked about how we sanctioned North Korea financially. What we did was we advised U.S. financial institutions to be wary of business with a particular bank, and that then created a ripple effect that you described where many other banks that had North Korean accounts decided, well, we are going to freeze these, or we are going to investigate them.

Bank presidents, regulators all started to target these accounts, and it had the effect of completely shutting North Korea off from the international financial system. They could not do a wire transfer. They could not access bank accounts through ATMs. It was really quite a powerful and forceful thing.

And in answer to your question, yes, I think that we can do that again. North Korea has since tried to adjust, but at the same time they still are able to operate in the financial system, and there are things that we can do to make that much more difficult.

Mr. ROHRABACHER. Are we talking about bank accounts that are being controlled and who operate for the benefit of the leadership of—specific leaders of North Korea and decisionmakers there?

Mr. CHA. I can't give you the answer to that question here. What I can say is that when that action happened, the North Korean negotiators, when they came back to the negotiation table, had only one demand, and that was to unfreeze the $25 million that was sitting in that bank in Macao. They did not want to talk about anything else under the sun. They didn't want to talk about peace treaty. They didn't want to talk about anything else. All they wanted to talk about was that, which gives you a sense of how important it was to them.

Mr. ROHRABACHER. Do the other witnesses have any comment on that?

Ms. GLASER. Congressman, I think that this also takes us back to the issue of China where there are so many of these small banks that exist along the border, and sometimes they shut down and they pop up someplace else, maybe even, you know, half a mile down the road.

There are some journalists who have gotten into some of these banks and pretended to make transactions just to demonstrate how easy it is to transfer money to North Korea. So, again, this goes back to the issue you raised earlier of shutting down these banking transactions, putting sanctions on these banks.

It is just essential to get the Chinese to comply with the sanctions that are already on the books that the Chinese have supported in the United Nations. And when it comes to things like luxury goods, just inspections along a border, they are episodic. There are times that the Chinese appear to want to signal the North Koreans that they are dissatisfied with something, and then they go back to business as usual.

Mr. KLINGNER. If I could just add, we talk about Chinese resistance, the Chinese Government resistance to actions. But we can actually get Chinese banks to work in our interests. With the Banco Delta Asia issue, as I mentioned before, the U.S. sent officials throughout Asia, including to the Bank of China, to talk and point out that under Section 311 they could face seizure of their assets in the United States and be precluded from accessing the U.S. financial system, which really is the kiss of death for any financial institution.

Even though the Chinese Government was urging the Chinese banks to resist any pressure, the banks themselves had to worry about their own reputational risk, their own access to the international system. So they complied. They severed—Bank of China, for example, severed its relationship with North Korea, even if the Chinese Government didn't want it, but they had to take those actions themselves to maintain, you know, the Bank of China as an entity.

Mr. ROHRABACHER. Thank you.

Thank you, Mr. Chairman.

Mr. SALMON. Thank you very much.

Mr. Connolly.

Mr. CONNOLLY. Thank you, Mr. Chairman, and welcome to our panel. I begin by taking issue with the ranking member's narrative with respect to Iran in comparing it to North Korea. My narrative would be that this administration took up from the neglect and fecklessness of the previous administration with respect to Iran. And, whether you like it or not, the agreement, the nuclear agreement, is working. They are complying.

And if you want to remove an existential threat to Israel, that is the way we did it, and it is—you know, in my view, it has the best probability of working of any solution offered on the table. Maybe one doesn't like that. Maybe one would have preferred a different alternative. But this is the one the United States Government pursued. I am glad they did. And I think in the long run it will be the best alternative for peace in the region and for taking the nuclear option with respect to Iran off the table.

Now, one of the pieces of leverage we had, in addition to sanctions, was choking off Iran's ability to sell the one product it really has, and that is oil. When it comes to North Korea, we don't have an analogous situation other than weapons. I am not quite sure what it is the North Koreans really have to sell that we can choke off.

Would that be a fair statement, Ms. Glaser?

Ms. GLASER. Yes. Yes, I would agree with you, Congressman. I don't know what North Korea has to sell that we can choke off, but——

Mr. CONNOLLY. But that is a real big difference between—I mean, to analogize North Korea and Iran, I just think is apples and oranges, because start with the fact that Iran has got oil; North Korea doesn't have anything, other than maybe weapons.

Ms. GLASER. There are some very important differences, of course, between North Korea and Iran, beginning with the fact that North Korea has nuclear weapons and has tested them and Iran has not. But, at the same time, I would agree with the points that have been made by Bruce Klingner and Victor Cha that there are mechanisms that we have used, sanctions that we have used, executive authorities we have used, against Iran that exist that we have not used against North Korea.

So there are many more ways that we could pressure North Korea, that we have applied to Iran I believe fairly successfully, but have not applied to North Korea.

Mr. CONNOLLY. Well, let me ask that question, and I welcome Dr. Cha and Mr. Klingner, but it is a devil's advocate question. I am not promoting it, but is that the best way to try to restrain and shape North Korean behavior, tighten sanctions, tighten economic consequences, because they will have to scream ''uncle'' at some point? Is that really what history tells us about North Korea? Ms. Glaser? And then, the other—both of the other panelists are free to comment as well.

Ms. GLASER. My view is that it must be part of any strategy. In itself, if we are not offering North Korea some positive vision of the future, then pressure/sanctions are unlikely to work.

Mr. CONNOLLY. Alone.

Ms. GLASER. Alone.

Mr. CONNOLLY. Yes.

Ms. GLASER. But I believe that the United States, under this administration and prior administrations, had made it quite clear to North Korea that there are many things that we can put on the table, security assurances, assistance, diplomatic relations. There is such thing as a—if you want to call it a grand bargain.

The North Koreans are aware that there would be benefits for them if they give up their nuclear weapons. So pressure, by itself, of course will not work, but pressure/sanctions must be part of any strategy.

Mr. CONNOLLY. Dr. Cha? Mr. Klingner?

Mr. KLINGNER. Yes, I agree. And even though my comments today have focused on sanctions, when I have talked about these in other fora in the past, I have always emphasized the context that it is one instrument.

Mr. CONNOLLY. And not always an effective one.

Mr. KLINGNER. Right. Just as diplomacy has not been effective.

Mr. CONNOLLY. Right.

Mr. KLINGNER. So, we often get into a binary debate of sanctions versus engagement, and we need both. I mean, it is part of a comprehensive integrated strategy. So we need continued offers of conditional engagement based on conditionality, reciprocity, transparency.

Unfortunately, we have had many agreements, four agreements, for them never to pursue nuclear weapons, and then four agreements to give up the weapons they promised never to build in the first place. Additional pressure, and then also those two tracks we hope will convince North Korea to alter its behavior, and then you also need the third track of having to ensure that you have sufficient defenses for yourself and your allies.

But when people say sanctions don't work because North Korea hasn't cut up its weapons, well, diplomacy was equally unable to do that. But sanctions have a number of other purposes. One is to enforce U.S. law. Two is to impose a penalty, a cost or pain when someone violates our law or international law or U.N. resolutions, and hopefully a deterrent to other would-be violators.

Three is to put into place mechanisms to impede the inflow of prohibited items, components for their nuclear missile programs, and the money from illicit activities. Four, to prevent or at least constrain proliferation. And, five, the most difficult, is to alter their behavior.

I would argue on four of the five that they have had some success.

Mr. CONNOLLY. Thoughtful. Thank you.

Dr. Cha.

Mr. CHA. Okay. Very quickly, Congressman, on the question about, what do they export that is of value? I mean, truly, what is of value to them? And so a couple of things come to mind in addition to the things that Bruce has already talked about.

One, as I mentioned before, is this issue of slave labor. That is providing income to them. It is something that is clearly in violation of ILO standards, even though they are not a signatory to the ILO, and that is certainly one area where it is not Iranian oil, but it is something that certainly is of value to them.

The other is there are a lot of raw materials actually in North Korea, and China since 2008 has extracted a lot of that for their two inland provinces. And when people are in Pyongyang, the capital city of North Korea, they say things look pretty good there now. That is all because of Chinese money from these contracts, and that is another area.

On the diplomacy side, I don't think anybody on this panel is against diplomacy. I think we all believe diplomacy is important, but I have to say that having been—having participated in negotiations for the last agreements with North Korea, the nuclear agreements, and knowing a lot about the Clinton administration agreements and President Obama's, we have put—I mean, as Bonnie said, they know what they get. We put everything on the table.

And the issue right now is that this young leader is not interested, and he is looking to build his programs because he wants to confront the next administration here.

Mr. CONNOLLY. Yes. If the chair would allow me one more question, and I will try to ask Ms. Glaser to be brief. But talk a little bit more about—it seems to me the one sort of inflection point we have got, if we have got leverage on North Korea, it is through China. It is in our relationship with China and their relationship with Pyongyang.

How much leverage do the Chinese really have? Because from a distance it looks like the Chinese are in a conundrum themselves. They have got relationships they don't want to walk away from. They don't want to even unwittingly destabilize the peninsula and have to deal with that mess. I mean, if you gave them truth serum, they would probably love a peaceful reunification organized by the south. But that is so far away, you know, they can't really effectuate that.

So how much leverage do the Chinese have, and how well are we pressuring them to try to effectuate better behavior from the North Koreans?

Ms. GLASER. Well, the Chinese, as I said in my earlier remarks, have enormous potential leverage. They are unwilling to use it. And because the Chinese are fearful of instability in North Korea, the leverage they have in essence becomes North Korea's leverage over them. Kim Jong Un and even his father I think have done quite a good job of playing a very weak hand, not only with the United States and other countries but particularly with China.

And so the North Koreans I think occasionally cause trouble for China in a variety of ways along the border, and in terms of the threats that they make toward South Korea. The Chinese need I think to be motivated to use the pressure that they have, and I don't think we have done a very good job of doing that.

I agree that we should not be self-deterred in putting pressure on China. We should not be worried that if we put pressure on China on this issue that they will somehow not cooperate with us on climate change, or Iran, for example. We can use pressure, if properly applied and well-timed, I think can have an impact on Chinese behavior.

And I would cite the example of when Xi Jinping was preparing to come to the United States last September, and the administration considered imposing cyber sanctions and had the executive authorities to do so. And the Chinese got very motivated to set up a new mechanism to send a standing member of the Politburo to discuss this issue.

Now, this may not in the end solve the problem of the cyber hacking and cyber-enabled theft, and I think we certainly have to keep their feet to the fire on that issue. But the point is that when you threaten sanctions, when you have the executive authorities to do so, and the Chinese take you seriously, that, yes, you can motivate their behavior.

There was also the discussion earlier about bolstering missile defense in the region, and I do think that taking steps that defend American interests and the interests of our allies, and if they happen to create a more negative security environment for China in the region, that may motivate the Chinese to do more as well. This is not something that they want to see. It doesn't benefit their interest.

Mr. CONNOLLY. I thank you very much.

Mr. Chairman, thank you for your indulgence.

Mr. SALMON. Mr. Connolly raised the issue that they don't really have much to export. Possibly they could export some cyber hacking training seminars.

The Chair recognizes Mr. DesJarlais.

Mr. DESJARLAIS. Thank you, Mr. Chairman, and thank you to our panel of witnesses for your thoughtful insight today. Dr. Cha, I wanted to ask you, do you believe that North Korea would use their nuclear weapons for aggressive actions?

Mr. CHA. I don't think it is the intent of any nuclear weapon state, including North Korea, to use them purposely for aggressive purposes. Having said that, there are easily contingencies one can imagine where a country, especially North Korea, can miscalculate. And I can draw out some of those scenarios for you in which they have no intent to use nuclear weapons, but because of military calculations they are then compelled to. And that is what is so inherently destabilizing about the current situation.

Mr. DESJARLAIS. I just want to talk a little bit about perception. I have not been to South Korea. I have not been to Japan. Do South Koreans and Japanese feel the same threat from North Korea that, say, Israel does with Iran?

Mr. CHA. I certainly think that Japan feels mortally threatened by the developments in North Korea, their missile program as well as their nuclear program. It is the clearest existential threat to Japan today.

With regard to South Korea, they have always been under the fear of artillery attack from North Korea. Artillery tubes are only seconds away from the capital city of Seoul. And I think there is now a growing concern about the broader nuclear question.

Again, if you have been under conventional military threat, bio-chemical, artillery shells, all your life, you can get a little jaded. But I think that there is a growing concern about the broader strategic implications of North Korea's nuclear program.

Mr. DESJARLAIS. Okay. And I am going somewhere with this. My sense is that, you know, here in this country we have a country, the only one in this century, testing nuclear weapons, detonate a nuclear weapon a week ago. But after the news comes out, it is like, oh, well, it wasn't a thermonuclear weapon; it was just a fission weapon, and, therefore, we don't need to worry about it.

We are having a hearing today, but I will tell you that every Member of Congress understands the threat Israel feels from Iran. It is something that Israel has done to raise that perception, and I think that everyone has learned to respect that threat. And I am not sure that is the same with North Korea.

And, you know, maybe our problem is that we need to raise that perception. Every Member of Congress, Democrat or Republican, generally takes a trip to Israel when they first go to Congress, and they see and they feel that threat. You know, maybe that is something Japan and something South Korea and other nations that feel threatened in the region should do to help increase that perception here in Congress, because honestly right now, I mean, you hear the news about Syria, you hear the news about ISIS, you hear about the Iran deal. It is sucking up all the oxygen, and that is what people are paying attention to.

So you all have a lot of great ideas of what to do, but how do we get action? And that is, you know, why we are here today. So, in your opinion, what do we do to elevate the reality that this is a real threat? Because it just—I have been sitting here with my colleague, Mr. Perry, talking about, you know, this problem should just be solved, but yet it is not happening.

And it doesn't seem that hard, but apparently it is. So what would you suggest? And I will give each of the panelists a chance to respond, 30 seconds each.

Mr. CHA. So I would entirely agree with you, Congressman, that I think outside of this chamber, more broadly in the American public, there is a tendency to downgrade, discount, dismiss North Korean activities as basically a crazy regime that blows up bombs in a cave somewhere near China, and that we don't have to worry about that, and I think that is completely the wrong attitude.

In part, it has been because there was a feeling that the United States sometimes overreacted in the past to North Korean actions and played into their hand. I think we are now in a period in which we are underreacting, and I think that is very dangerous.

Mr. DesJarlais. Thank you.

Mr. Klingner.

Mr. KLINGNER. North Korea is easy to ridicule, and it is easy to make the butt of jokes, as members of the panel have pointed out. It is a very real threat, a nuclear threat, a biological/chemical threat, that conventional forces, cyber threat, human rights threat, it runs the gamut, and it is not only against our allies, but increasingly to the United States.

Last year three U.S. four-star commanders said that North Korea has a nuclear weapon that could hit the United States today. They must know something. A year or so ago, South Korean press had a lot of articles from defectors about Kim Jong Un had directed a new war plan be implemented after—or created after he came into office, so that North Korea could take over the peninsula in 7 days before the U.S. could flow reinforcements there. That would require, as directed in that war plan, the use of nuclear weapons. It is a real threat.

Mr. DesJarlais. Thank you.

Ms. Glaser.

Ms. GLASER. It is also disheartening to me that there is an underappreciation for how much of a threat North Korea's nuclear weapons poses, and of course Israel does such a terrific job in Congress and in the American public at large, I think more can be done in the area of public education, and certainly hearings such as this and on North Korea's human rights record I think would be very important in highlighting this issue.

More actions up at the United Nations as well to get more people involved in this discussion. Help people to understand that we need to really—to dissect what the threat is, see that it is increasingly an existential threat, and not just put this on the back burner. So I completely agree with—I share your concern.

Mr. DesJarlais. I thank the panel, and thank you, Chairman.

Mr. SALMON. Thank you.

Ms. Gabbard.

Ms. GABBARD. Thank you, Mr. Chairman. I appreciate Mr. DesJarlais bringing up this issue and each of you expressing your shared concerns about this underappreciation and really a lack of understanding about the threat. I represent Hawaii's 2nd District here. And as you can imagine, being out there in the middle of the Pacific, every time North Korea starts making threats, launching these tests, this is something knowing, as you said, Mr. Klingner, Hawaii and the west coast, at a minimum, already are within range of North Korea's capabilities, both of an ICBM as well as a nuclear weapon.

So this is something that really rings true and is deeply understood by folks in my state who recognize the need for stronger missile defense, who recognize the need for taking this threat with the seriousness that it deserves.

I have got a few questions. The sanctions bill that we passed yesterday, particularly as it relates to hard currency, do you believe that it will have the same effect as in 2005 when it was first put in place? For whomever would like to answer.

Mr. CHA. I think the bill is great, and I think that the mechanism is still there to carry out the same sorts of targeted financial sanctioning. North Korea, since 2005, has tried to circumvent this. But, again, a lot of it depends on what entities we choose to sanction, what individuals we choose to target, and Chinese compliance with that.

Having said that, I can easily imagine things that we can do that would not collapse the U.S.-China relationship or, as Mr. Sherman said earlier, not have a major effect on Wall Street. So there is plenty of room to operate.

Ms. GABBARD. That will directly impact their pocketbooks.

Mr. CHA. Yes.

Ms. GABBARD. So along those lines, I mean, look back to what happened in 2005 and what led to their agreement in 2007 when those sanctions were lifted.

I would just like to hear your thoughts on what you see is a viable path forward should that end be reached, should these sanctions be so effective that we get to a point where we have got an opportunity there, understanding, really, that North Korea sees their nuclear program as an insurance policy against regime change, seeing what they learned from what happened in Libya with Gaddafi, and really what caused their—I think that window, frankly, to close, where they wouldn't trust—that if there was an agreement to denuclearize that the United States wouldn't go after them to try to implement the regime change.

So I would just like to hear your thoughts on engagement with North Korea and how understanding this climate there is a path forward.

Mr. KLINGNER. Just commenting on yesterday's bill, it closes a number of loopholes. It elevates a number of existing executive orders or regulations to legislation giving it additional power. It makes a number of implementations mandatory rather than discretionary. So I think it has—will provide a number of benefits to the U.S. effort.

But the bill, as well as existing measures, it is dependent on the implementation and our willingness to use the powers we already have. Last year the executive order that was released in January allows the U.S. to sanction North Korean officials simply for being North Korean officials. We don't even have to provide evidence that they have conducted illegal activity. That gives us tremendous power. The U.S. sanctioned 16 Russian officials for being Russian officials after the Crimea incursion. We haven't used that power as much as we could.

The target has changed. Banco Delta Asia was very effective because it was a very large conduit. North Korea has adapted since then. But it is sort of like the cockroach theory of law enforcement.

You go into a kitchen, you turn on the light, you see where the cockroaches are, and where they run off to. If you take out the first node, the Plan A of North Korea, you then alert your intelligence and law enforcement authorities, so they watch where the money gets redirected, where the cockroaches go.

Ms. GABBARD. Right.

Mr. KLINGNER. It is then you go after the Plan B.

Ms. GABBARD. Right.

Ms. GLASER. On the issue of engagement, Congressman, as we talked about earlier, we have to have a strategy that deals with— that is composed of engagement as well as coercive steps. As far as I understand, the United States engages with North Korea. We have the channel in New York. We do talk to the North Koreans.

But I think we have to be careful about agreeing to revive, you know, the Six Party talks mechanism, as the Chinese often encourage us to do, in the absence of some return to the commitments that the North Koreans made under the 2005 and other agreements.

Now, the North Koreans want to engage in dialogue so that they can get a peace treaty and be recognized as a nuclear weapon state. I think that is a bad outcome for the United States and our interests and our allies.

So we have to engage North Korea in a way that they understand that there are steps that they have to take. They have to go back to these commitments of giving up nuclear weapons. And if they are willing to go ahead with a freeze as a first step toward— with the understanding that the goal is that they eventually give them up, then I think the United States has always been willing to work with that.

I don't think there are signs that under Kim Jong Un that the North Koreans are willing to engage in serious negotiations with the end goal of denuclearizing the peninsula. So I think that engagement, yes, but we have to be careful about how we use it.

Ms. GABBARD. Thank you.

Thank you, Mr. Chairman, for holding this hearing and for continuing to help increase awareness on North Korea's threat.

Mr. SALMON. Thank you very much.

The Chair recognizes Brigadier General Perry.

Mr. PERRY. Congressman Perry will be fine. Thank you. Thanks to the chairman. Thanks to the panel.

A list of questions here, maybe just all at once, and if you would comment, you know. I understand that we are reportedly in talks with South Korea regarding the reintroduction of nuclear weapons, United States' nuclear weapons onto the peninsula. What is the status of that, if you know? Why wouldn't South Korea be interested?

Regarding the introduction of THAAD, the missile defense interceptor system, why not? Is South Korea concerned that it would be too provocative? Why wouldn't they want that?

Regarding curtailing conventional arms sales, how would that be done? Again, you know, I have been listening, as everybody else has, the whole time saying, "Why aren't we doing this?" And you folks are the experts and you don't know, but maybe you can give me some insight into that.

And regarding increasing the pressure on their human rights atrocities, which are just unimaginable to me, what is the best way? What is the best way to do that? And from my standpoint, I, like you folks, don't understand at all why we are not imposing these financial sanctions out of hand, like with your morning coffee. To me, the President should just sign that and on with—and move on to the next terrain feature, but that is my perception.

What would be the response to some of these things from our allies and trading partners in the region? Thank you.

Mr. CHA. I will take a piece of those, and then I will look to Bruce to take other pieces of it. In terms of the why, you know, why haven't we done more question, one aspect of this is China, and we have had a very full discussion on that. I think the other part of it is that it is priority and commitment.

This has not been a priority, unfortunately, even though, as I said, it is a very dangerous situation. And there has to be a political commitment to make the North Korean regime feel like there are costs to their behavior. There has been a political commitment to create the machinery, but there hasn't been a political commitment to implement.

I think part of the reason there hasn't been that is that there has always been some hope that there is a chance for diplomacy, like with Iran, like with Cuba, or like with Myanmar. But I am of the view that we are not going to see any diplomacy until the end of this administration.

Mr. PERRY. If I can interrupt you, is there a downside risk? Because I don't see a whole lot of downside risk. I understand that there is no commitment to going the upside, and you might expend some capital or whatever. I just don't see any—like what do we lose by doing this?

Mr. CHA. Well, I think the primary downside has to do with China and the relationship with China. At least that is the perceived downside. And then there is a degree of inertia. I think there really is a degree of inertia, because this is an issue traditionally that administrations want to put on the shelf. They don't necessarily want to commit to solve it. They want to put it on the shelf.

And so there is almost a pattern to this. They do a provocation, we issue a statement, we slap a sanction on them, and everybody goes back to dealing with other issues. And that is a rapidly deteriorating situation.

Mr. KLINGNER. If I could address them in reverse order. On human rights atrocities, as I have included in my statement, a number of cases where we have imposed sanctions and measures on other countries for their human rights violations but not North Korea, we have the authority to do so, obviously. We have done it to other countries. And also, the executive order of last January, which gives us the authority to sanction someone for being a member of the government.

You know, tomorrow with his morning coffee the President could add 50 North Korean entities, including Kim Jong Un by name, as well as every agency named in the U.N. Commission of Inquiry report, as well as the heads of all of those agencies. I don't know why we don't do that.

Curtailing conventional arms sales—the U.N. resolutions not only cover the nuclear and missile programs, they also prevent trade on conventional arms. There have been at least three interceptions of conventional arms shipments from North Korea to other nations, but apparently in the resolution sanction-busting hierarchy, they are not worth enforcing because they didn't even convene U.N. meetings about those violations.

So one thing we should be pushing for at the U.N. is Chapter 7, Clause 42 authority, which allows military enforcement of the U.N. resolutions. That doesn't mean attack, it doesn't mean invasion, but it provides the authority for, say, Coast Guard interception of ships.

We have had cases where the U.S. warships have been trailing North Korean freights for hundreds of miles, because we didn't have the authority to board or inspect them. On THAAD, I can send you a copy of my report on THAAD, South Korea has been hesitant, I believe, because of Chinese pressure and economic blackmail.

But last night during a major speech President Park Geun-hye, I think for the first time her administration said they want to discuss with the United States the possible deployment of THAAD to the peninsula.

And reintroducing nuclear weapons, that is very contentious. Both the U.S. and South Korean Governments have said they don't see a military necessity of putting U.S. nuclear weapons on the ground in South Korea, because we have sea-based and air-based weapons which can do the job and wouldn't provide a sort of pre-emptive target in South Korea for North Korea.

Ms. GLASER. If I could just add briefly, Congressman, President Park has attached a great deal of priority to China, hopes to gain China's support ultimately for reunification, but also in the near term for putting more pressure on China. And I agree with my colleagues that I think that is the main issue with THAAD. I don't think that President Park is unmovable on this issue, and with the growing threat she may agree.

But the Chinese seek to weaken U.S. alliances, and this is a major problem in trying to deal with the North Korea problem. Unless we can have a bigger strategy with the Chinese, make this a priority, and perhaps give China some of the reassurances that Congressman Sherman was talking about earlier, if we really have a reunified peninsula and we don't need to necessarily have troops along China's border.

The Chinese are very concerned, though, that the situation could be far more detrimental to them today than—in the future than it is today.

I also think there is an issue with the United States giving China credit for very small steps it takes—for example, supporting a U.N. Security Council Resolution—that it has diluted, prevented the application, for example, of economic sanctions, banking sanctions, just because the United States wants to isolate North Korea, and that is a valuable goal.

Yes, we should seek to isolate North Korea, but at the same time we should be putting far greater pressure on China to do more. And the Chinese believe that the United States is not prioritizing this issue. They see us as having put this on the back burner, and so little incentive for them to attach a priority to it either.

Mr. PERRY. Yes. I think we just continue to reward bad behavior. And as much as the Chinese are I think doing a delicate dance with their economy and their political system, at the end of the day I think that it serves their purpose to have North Korea remain communist or totalitarian. They are communists at their heart, and that is what they want to maintain.

And with all due respect to South Korea and the President, I understand what she is trying to get to. But at their heart, they are communists, and that is who they are.

But thank you, Mr. Chairman, for the hearing.

Mr. SALMON. I would like to really thank the panel members. I think that this has been an incredibly productive hearing.

Congressman Perry, you asked a lot of questions I think that a lot of us have been entertaining ourselves. You know, a lot of the whys, why—you know, is North Korea less of a threat than they were several years ago when there was tons of media attention and concern across America. And just 3 short years ago in the Presidential debates it was front and center, one of the most important issues of our time.

And the only thing that kind of comes to mind is an old adage, if a tree falls in the forest and nobody hears it, did it make a sound? And we just haven't focused the attention—when I say ''we,'' I don't think it has been a priority for the last 3 years.

Mr. PERRY. The question I have is, what is it going to take?

Mr. SALMON. Well——

Mr. PERRY. And that is scary.

Mr. SALMON. And I think that is why we are here today, because in the absence of leadership on this issue I think that that realm falls to us, that we have a responsibility then to stand up and try to take matters into our hands, whether it is trying to influence South Korea on THAAD, or whether it is looking at potential new sanctions or, at the very least, redeclaring North Korea a terrorist state.

There are lots of options I think that are on the table, and that is the reason that we did the hearing today, not just to shine light, not just to talk, but I think our goal is to try to put together legislation—a bill or several bills—that will try to move us in the right direction.

And my intention is to work with the panelists to try to craft that legislation and mark it up for a full committee hearing, because while other parts of the globe are in jeopardy, that doesn't diminish the threat that this part of the globe holds. And just because we are not paying attention to it doesn't mean that it is not a serious threat.

And I think that it is time that we focus our attentions on this serious, serious, serious issue that poses a threat to not just our national security, our allies in national security, but global national security. The threat of a nut job like Kim Jong Un having deployment capabilities with a nuclear weapon is incredibly frightening.

I think one of the things we didn't talk about today, what about the possibility—even if it is remote, what about the possibility of a partnership between North Korea and Iran? With all the money that Iran now has, or will have, and nuclear capabilities in North Korea, what about the possibility of joining forces to become an uber threat to everything that we hold dear.

So I think that this hearing is not an ending place. It is a beginning place for what needs to take our attention. I think, Mr. Chairman, you wanted to make a comment.

Mr. SHERMAN. As to our attention, they say in journalism if it bleeds, it leads. The Middle East, therefore, gets the attention, and it deserves some attention. But this North Korean problem is a threat to Asia and the United States.

And then as to the possible connection between North Korea and Iran, we need an agreement with China that there are no nonstop flights between North Korea and Iran. They would all go over Chinese airspace. We don't have to make a big political deal, just inform the planes that if they want to fly over your airspace, they have got to stop in a Chinese city for refueling. It would be unsafe for them to go that extra mile all the way without stopping for refueling. And if that happens, I am sure the Chinese will take a look at the plane. If we don't have that, the money is there on the one hand, the desire for nuclear weapons, and the 12th—the 13th nuclear weapon goes on eBay.

I yield back.

Mr. SALMON. I think what is really clear is that we have to break outside the existing paradigm, and the status quo is not working. And so we have to be creative and start coming up with some maybe old ideas with oomph or some new ideas, and I am open.

And so thank you very much for the panelists. Thank you, Ranking Member, and the committee members as well.

This meeting is now adjourned.

[Whereupon, at 10:49 a.m., the subcommittee was adjourned.]

A P P E N D I X

MATERIAL SUBMITTED FOR THE RECORD

SUBCOMMITTEE HEARING NOTICE
COMMITTEE ON FOREIGN AFFAIRS
U.S. HOUSE OF REPRESENTATIVES
WASHINGTON, DC 20515-6128

Subcommittee on Asia and the Pacific
Matt Salmon (R-AZ), Chairman

January 13, 2016

TO: MEMBERS OF THE COMMITTEE ON FOREIGN AFFAIRS

You are respectfully requested to attend an OPEN hearing of the Committee on Foreign Affairs, to be held by the Subcommittee on Asia and the Pacific in Room 2172 of the Rayburn House Office Building (and available live on the Committee website at http://www.ForeignAffairs.house.gov):

DATE: Wednesday, January 13, 2016

TIME: 9:00 a.m.

SUBJECT: The U.S. Response to North Korea's Nuclear Provocations

WITNESSES: Victor Cha, Ph.D.
Senior Adviser and Korea Chair
Center for Strategic and International Studies

Mr. Bruce Klingner
Senior Research Fellow for Northeast Asia
The Heritage Foundation

Ms. Bonnie Glaser
Senior Adviser for Asia
Director of China Power Project
Center for Strategic and International Studies

By Direction of the Chairman

The Committee on Foreign Affairs seeks to make its facilities accessible to persons with disabilities. If you are in need of special accommodations, please call 202/225-5021 at least four business days in advance of the event, whenever practicable. Questions with regard to special accommodations in general (including availability of Committee materials in alternative formats and assistive listening devices) may be directed to the Committee.

COMMITTEE ON FOREIGN AFFAIRS

MINUTES OF SUBCOMMITTEE ON _____Asia and the Pacific_____ HEARING

Day__ _Wednesday_ __ Date__ _January 13th, 2016_ __Room_____ _2172_____

Starting Time ____ _9:02am_____ Ending Time __ _10:49am___

Recesses |__-__| (____to ____) (____to ____) (____to ____) (____to ____) (____to ____) (____to ____)

Presiding Member(s)

Matt Salmon

Check all of the following that apply:

Open Session ☑   Electronically Recorded (taped) ☐
Executive (closed) Session ☐   Stenographic Record ☐
Televised ☐

TITLE OF HEARING:

The U.S. Response to North Korea's Nuclear Provocations

SUBCOMMITTEE MEMBERS PRESENT:

Dana Rohrabacher, Steve Chabot, Scott Perry, Scott DesJarlais
Brad Sherman, Ami Bera, Alan Lowenthal, Gerald Connolly, Grace Meng

---

NON-SUBCOMMITTEE MEMBERS PRESENT: _(Mark with an * if they are not members of full committee.)_

~

HEARING WITNESSES: Same as meeting notice attached? Yes ☑ No ☐
(If "no", please list below and include title, agency, department, or organization.)

-

STATEMENTS FOR THE RECORD: _(List any statements submitted for the record.)_

    Gerald Connolly

TIME SCHEDULED TO RECONVENE ____-____
or
TIME ADJOURNED ____ _10:49am_____

                             Subcommittee Staff Director

Statement for the Record
Submitted by Mr. Connolly of Virginia

Displays of military strength by the U.S. and our allies, repeated multilateral diplomatic efforts, United Nations Security Council resolutions, and a robust sanctions regime have proven insufficient in deterring North Korea from further developing its illicit nuclear weapons program or improving human rights conditions for its people.

North Korea is a reckless, paranoid state devoid of basic autonomy for its citizens. The fact that such a regime is armed with a nuclear umbrella makes the Korean Peninsula one of the most dangerous flashpoints in the globe. It also begs the questions – what are our policy and strategic options in addressing this confounding threat, and where is our leverage in moving North Korea towards denuclearization?

On January 6, 2016, North Korea conducted its fourth nuclear weapons test and confirmed for the world, once again, its preference for defying international norms and risking the destabilization of the Asia-Pacific region.

In the immediate wake of this profoundly disturbing provocation, I welcomed the timely, if not overdue, consideration and passage of the North Korea Sanctions Enforcement Act (H.R. 757) by the House of Representatives. By targeting the individuals and entities that support the Kim regime through illicit activities, the legislation will help weaken the resolve and capability of Pyongyang to endanger regional stability. As the Administration has stated that its North Korea policy includes deterrence, diplomacy, and pressure, this legislation demonstrates that Congress will support an important pillar of that strategy and apply pressure to Pyongyang through sanctions.

The nuclear test - which North Korea claimed was a hydrogen bomb despite seismic readings to the contrary - is not the only recent weapons advancement North Korea has announced or demonstrated. It also publicized a submarine launched ballistic missile on December 21, 2015 and has put on parade a KN-08 road-mobile intercontinental ballistic missile. Either capability, if operational, would significantly complicate U.S. nuclear deterrence calculations against North Korea. Furthermore, it is estimated that North Korea could have more than 50 nuclear weapons by the end of the decade.

As a co-chair of the Congressional Caucus on Korea, I remain deeply concerned that any new development or growth in North Korea's nuclear weapons program only exacerbates the volatility and ever-present potential of conflict on the Korean Peninsula. It is a specter that looms over 75 million Koreans, and – for their sake and that of the region – the U.S., the Republic of Korea (R.O.K.), China and other regional stakeholders must demonstrate our shared commitment to addressing and eliminating this threat.

Current U.S. policy towards North Korea has been characterized as "deterrence, diplomacy, and pressure to make clear that North Korea will not achieve security or prosperity while it pursues nuclear weapons, abuses its own people, and flouts its longstanding obligations and commitments." If the carrot we have extended to North Korea – and by extension China's interests on the Peninsula – is security and prosperity in exchange for denuclearization and improved human rights protections, it seems that the basis of any ultimate resolution must be both a shared understanding of what constitutes "security and prosperity" as well as complete clarity regarding the ability of the U.S. to deliver that incentive. Currently, the U.S., China, and North Korea do not have a shared definition of what constitutes security and prosperity on the Korean Peninsula and Chinese officials have said as much since January 6th. This lack of common understanding of a basic tenet of U.S. policy significantly erodes the effectiveness or applicability of this "carrot."

The alternative to this carrot is, of course, the stick. Further economic sanctions, international isolation, and the military capability of the U.S., the R.O.K. and our allies have been clearly demonstrated to Pyongyang, but have not resulted in any significant change in the behavior of North Korea. The ultimate disincentive, regime collapse, while supremely feared by both North Korea and China, also has significant security implications for the R.O.K. and other regional allies of the U.S. However, the instability of the Kim regime dictates that the region should gird itself for this possibility as such an outcome would likely be rapid and without significant advanced warning.

With incentives and disincentives in U.S. North Korea policy lacking effective implementation or demonstrated results, it is clear that the U.S. must address these deficiencies or explore creative policy alternatives and bold action on arresting and eliminating the North Korean nuclear program. It is not the case that we can allow this threat to languish and hope that it does not result in disaster. The potential for harm is too great.